Over The Top:

How The Internet Is (Slowly But Surely) Changing The Television Industry

Alan Wolk

DEDICATION

*This book is dedicated to my children, Arik and Miriam,
who make everything possible and everything worthwhile.*

Table of Contents

ACKNOWLEDGMENTS

I want to thank everyone who has been with me on this journey and whose insights and encouragement made this all possible. In alphabetical order: Ivan Askwith, Michele Band, David Beck, Alex Blum, Eoin Dowling, Alan Dybner, Guy Finley, Field Garthwaite, Rich Greenfield, Gale Harold, Tarley Jordan, Scott Lowell, Jeff MacIntyre, Chuck Parker, Jesse Redniss, Brian Ring, Natasha Roberton, Anthony Rose, Seth Shapiro, Gunther Sonnenfeld, Robert Tercek, Jeremy Toeman, Zane Vella, Andrew Wallenstein, David Williams, Hilary Wolk, and David Zaslav

ALAN WOLK

PREFACE

THE LAST MEDIUM TO BE DISRUPTED BY THE INTERNET

Television is the last of the twentieth-century mass media to be disrupted by the twenty-first century internet. It's also going to prove to be the toughest. The American television industry is still a cash machine that's protected by an intricate web of rights deals and inertia. But that's changing, and rapidly. And when it does, it's going to change the industry dramatically, making it even better for both creators and consumers.

In the first section of this book, we'll examine where the industry is today: who the players are, how they interact with each other (who pays who and for what), and what their sweet spots and pain points are.

Next, we'll look at a number of current trends that are starting to rock the industry, looking at both the business and technology aspects of each and what their road map for the next few years looks like.

Finally, we'll end with some predictions about where the industry ends up, who the winners and losers are and what TV will look like in the coming decades.

Sit back and enjoy the ride.

SECTION 1

The Television Industry Today:
A Primer For The Uninformed

ALAN WOLK

The Players

PLAYER #1: THE NETWORKS

The networks (ABC, CBS, MTV, et al.) provide content, and right now they are the most powerful force in the industry. They are traditionally broken down as follows:

- Broadcast Networks (ABC, CBS, NBC, PBS, FOX and the CW)
- Cable Networks (Discovery, A&E, ESPN, The Weather Channel, MTV, et al.)

These distinctions were much more important thirty years ago during the early days of the cable industry. But today, with pay TV penetration approaching 90% in the U.S., the larger cable networks tend to draw the same ratings as broadcast networks and, just as importantly, viewers—especially younger viewers who came of age with cable as a given—don't really see a distinction. Nonetheless there are business model differences, which are addressed below.

How Do They Make Money?
Networks have two revenue streams: ad sales and content deals.

Ad Sales. Networks sell national advertising on their shows; local advertising is sold by the carriers, or, in the case of broadcast networks, by the local affiliates (independently owned broadcast stations.) Ad revenue has been dropping slightly over the past several years, largely, many believe, due to a phenomenon known as time-shifting: people record their favorite shows and then watch them at their leisure. (In fact, a recent Piksel study showed that only 11% of respondents exclusively watch their favorite shows live, versus 57% who exclusively watch them time-shifted.)

NIELSEN. The A.C. Nielsen company has long been the established source for television ratings in the U.S. Ratings were initially established so that advertisers would know which programs had the most viewers, which in turn affected the amount the networks could charge for ads on that particular show. Nielsen also provided demographic data based on households. Back in the days when there were only three networks, the race for ratings was paramount, and the "overnights"—Nielsen's next-day ratings—were critical.

But the industry has changed radically over the past few years (hence this book) and Nielsen has come under a lot of fire lately for not changing with the times. At a time when other digital media are able to accurately measure every single view, Nielsen still relies on a small sampling of households who are tasked with recording their viewing habits in a diary (in pre-internet days, this was an actual handwritten diary). It's a system that seems wildly outdated in 2015, when the MVPDs can look at their set-top boxes and accurately determine the exact number of people who are watching at any given time; yet no one on either side (advertisers or networks) seems ready to completely abandon it until something better is in place. Nielsen keeps promising to fix things, but can't seem to follow through; we've been waiting since January 2013 for their complete TV Everywhere ratings package.

The rapid shift away from live viewing has also lead to a dispute between the networks, Nielsen and the advertising agencies over what constitutes the right "window" for counting a show's viewership. Currently, shows are measured by what's known as "C3" or a three-day window from when the show first aired. (Nielsen includes DVR and VOD views in that number.)

Many would like to see that expanded to "C7" or one week from first airing, and in June of 2014 one of the major media buying agencies announced that they were indeed moving to C7, albeit only during prime time and only for the broadcast networks. A recent study by Rentrak, a Nielsen competitor, showed the huge C7 viewership for the show *Mad Men* and claimed that millions of dollars in ad revenue were being left on the table as a result, giving more fuel to the argument in favor of C7 ratings. (The counterargument says that viewers watching in that C4-C7 range are more likely to skip commercials and that the messages in those commercials may no longer be relevant.)

The networks seem to be moving in this direction as well, in January 2015, NBC Universal announced that all of their cable networks (Bravo, SyFy, USA, E! et al.) would be moving away from an L+SD (live + same day) to an L+3 (live + 3 days) system. Just a week earlier, Les Moonves, the CEO of CBS, said that overnight ratings were "worthless."

People are also watching a lot more television on their connected devices (smartphones and tablets.) While Nielsen has been working on a solution, none has been implemented to date, and views on those devices go uncounted. We'll take a closer look at OTT viewing—and how to measure it—later on.

Content Deals. Cable networks license their content to the various cable companies, satellite providers, and telcos (collectively known in the industry as MVPDs— Multichannel Video Programming Distributors). The price for these deals, commonly known as "carriage fees," is determined by the value of the network (number of viewers, potential revenue from local ad sales) multiplied by the number of subscribers the MVPD has. These deals are renegotiated every few years, which is why you sometimes see battles where, say, Verizon is threatening not to show AMC programming because the post-*Mad Men*/*Breaking Bad* AMC wants more money than Verizon is prepared to give them. Since it is not uncommon for carriage deals to be in place for five years or longer, a network that makes significant gains in viewership may have to wait several years to see the rewards.

Broadcast networks receive what is known as "retrans fees" from the MVPDs for the right to retransmit their programming to local stations. Retrans fees are quite hefty and the networks make billions of dollars (literally) from them.

Retrans fees were under fire before the U.S. Supreme Court made a ruling to shut down Aereo in a landmark case decided in June 2014. Aereo was a service that essentially rented two small antennas to a user. The antennas lived in an Aereo antenna farm and the programming they pulled in was sent via WiFi to the end user who then used the Aereo app to watch via a streaming device like Roku or on a smartphone or tablet. The networks sued Aereo claiming they were violating copyright laws by reselling something the networks were giving away for free. Aereo claimed that they were just renting antennae. But the real issue here was retrans. If the Supreme Court had ruled that Aereo was legal, there would have been nothing to stop the MVPDs from either teaming with Aereo or launching their own versions of the service. Either way, they'd have gotten around having to pay the networks billions of dollars in retrans fees. At which point the networks would have had two options: suck it up and find new revenue streams (unlikely) or pull the cord on actually broadcasting their content and delivering their programming via cable, which would allow them to collect carriage fees like the other cable networks.

BUNDLING: Here's where content deals get tricky: most of the larger networks own multiple channels. (See the chart on the following page for a full listing.) And they sell them to the MVPDs as an airtight package or bundle: You want ESPN? Well then you need to take the Badminton Channel and the Dodgeball Channel and all 30 of ESPN/Disney's other channels too. Right now, the MVPDs don't have much wiggle room since they compete with each other and not being able to offer ESPN to potential subscribers would put them at a huge disadvantage.

The networks also know that you probably have no interest in watching the Badminton Channel, so they forbid the MVPDs from letting you do things like making your "Favorite Channels" list the default view, lest you leave the Badminton Channel off of that list. Networks also pay to have a good spot in the channel line-up and so they're not about to give that up and let you, the viewer, start creating your own order—at least not as the default view. That may change as more dynamic program guides come into play, especially on tablet-based TV Everywhere line-ups. But for the moment, those TV set-based program guides remain static.

That means, contrary to popular belief, your pay TV provider is not the one forcing you to take thousand-channel bundled packages. The networks are more or less forcing them to offer it. The MVPDs would love to be able to sell unbundled packages since they'd make more money by signing up more subscribers while simultaneously cutting their own content acquisition costs.

The interface is the main pain point in today's TV viewing experience. That giant, unwieldy grid was designed for about seven channels and is now being forced to accommodate 700. A new interface would need to be free from the stranglehold of bundled content, which is why you haven't seen one yet. But look at XBox or Roku or Netflix for an idea of what's possible.

WHO OWNS WHAT: NETWORK BUNDLES
(JV = JOINT VENTURE)

ABC/DISNEY
ABC Television
ABC News
Fusion
A+E Networks (JV)
- A&E
- History
- Bio
- H2
- Military History
- Crime & Investigation
- Lifetime
- Lifetime Movie Network
- Lifetime Real Women

Disney Channel
Disney Cinemagic
Disney Junior
Disney XD
ESPN
ESPN2
ESPN on ABC
ESPN Classic

ESPNews
ESPN Deportes

CBS
CBS Television
CBS News
CBS Sports
The CW
Showtime
Showtime 2
Showtime Showcase
Showtime Extreme
Showtime Beyond
Showtime Next
Showtime Women
Showtime Family Zone
The Movie Channel
The Movie Channel Xtra
Smithsonian
TV Guide Network

NBC UNIVERSAL
Bravo
Chiller
Cloo
CNBC
E!
Esquire Channel
G4
MSNBC
Mun2
NBC
NBC Sports
Oxygen
PBS Kids Sprout
Syfy
Telemundo
The Golf Channel
The Weather Channel (JV)

TV One
Universal HD
USA Network

FOX
Big Ten Network (JV)
Fox Business Network
Fox College Sports
Fox Broadcasting
Fox News Channel
Fox Soccer Plus
Fox Sports 1
Fox Sports 2
Fox Sports Networks
FX
FXX
FX Movie Channel
National Geographic Channel (JV)
Nat Geo Mundo (JV)
Nat Geo Wild (JV)

VIACOM
BET
CMT
CMT Pure Country
Comedy Central
Logo
MTV
MTV2
MTV Hits
MTV Jams
mtvU
Nick at Nite
Nick Jr.
Nickelodeon
Nicktoons
Palladia
Spike
TeenNick

Tr3s
TV Land
VH1
VH1 Classic
VH1 Soul

OVERSEAS RIGHTS: The networks and studios also have an incredibly lucrative business selling their shows overseas; it's a win-win as those markets have a limited amount of home-grown content and economies of scale make it hard for them to rival U.S. production values. What's interesting here is that having licensed the content to a third party (the overseas distributor), the networks are much less concerned with things like TV Everywhere rights, which is one of the reasons why overseas markets are ahead of the U.S. in that regard.

O&Os AND AFFILIATES: The networks all have what are known as "O and Os"— owned and operated stations that they run themselves, usually in larger cities. These stations run the networks programming plus their own locally-oriented news shows, and all profits go directly to the network. Affiliates are independently owned stations that pay to run the networks programming. They are under no obligation to do so, and many typically buy the bulk of their programming from syndication services and only run the networks prime time schedule. Nonetheless, affiliate stations remain a significant revenue source for the broadcast networks.

.

PLAYER #2: THE MVPDS

Comcast, Uverse, DirectTV and the rest. The United States is one of the only countries where MVPDs are regional rather than national. (Though in light of the proposed Comcast-Time Warner merger, that may be changing.)

How Do They Make Money?
MVPDs have two revenue streams:
- Local Ad Sales on the programming they run
- Subscription fees from consumers

The vast majority of MVPDs don't just sell pay TV packages. They sell broadband and landline services too. The old "Triple Play." It's an incredibly lucrative system for them and an incredibly bulletproof one too.

HOW MANY CORDS CAN YOU CUT? It's bulletproof because what tech bloggers often forget when they talk about "cord cutting" is that the cord that brings you television is generally attached to the cord that brings you the internet. And if you're cutting the one, you're still going to need the other. (To put this in perspective, somewhere over 90% of FIOS and Uverse subscribers get TV and broadband from the same provider.) So here's where the genius of this set-up kicks in: the MVPDs will give you two options—get the pay TV service and get unlimited bandwidth (*free* unlimited bandwidth, in the case of Google Fiber), or, get broadband only, but face possible bandwidth caps. If you're a heavy TV watcher who plans to get content off web-based services like Netflix and Amazon, you probably won't wind up saving any money.

The MVPDs are not blind either. They see where the market is going, understand the effect of Netflix and Amazon. And so they are busy cutting deals to include those services in their offering. It's already happening in Kansas City, where Google Fiber TV has Netflix baked into the program guide with more OTT (Over The Top—the industry term for signals carried over the open internet) channels to come. Smaller MVPDs such as Atlantic Broadband, Grande Communications, and RCN recently announced deals to carry Netflix on their networks, and it won't be long until the larger players follow suit.

PLAYER #3: THE STUDIOS

While the networks do produce some of their own programming, many TV shows are produced by studios and production companies. These range from studios affiliated with the larger movie studios (Warner, 20th Century, Sony et al) to smaller, independent production companies like Amblin and Bad Robot. Every year studios option hundreds of scripts and winnow them down to the ones most likely to get picked up by cable and broadcast networks. Of these scripts, a dozen or two will get made into pilots in the hopes that they will get selected by one of the networks. Finally, the pilots are winnowed down by the network programming executives into the shows that will actually appear on air the following season. (This process is not set in stone and shows with big name stars or big name producers associated with them will often get picked up without having to go through much of the winnowing process.)

How Do They Make Money?
Studios make money when their programs are picked up by the networks. The networks pay them a fee to run the series and reap advertising revenue from it. Sometimes, if the producer is powerful, they can work a deal where they get a share of the ad revenue.

That's just step one.

If a series is successful (the holy grail has been 100 episodes, or around four or five seasons), the studio can then sell syndication rights to independent TV stations and networks like USA or TBS that rely on reruns of recent hit shows. Syndication is worth millions of dollars and can continue to line pockets for years.

In the past few years, Netflix and Amazon have become a key source of income for studios too, as they pay top dollar for full seasons of reruns, which allows for binge viewing. Studios and networks like this arrangement because, (a) it's very lucrative and (b) if the show is still on air, they can attract new viewers who have caught up via Netflix. Selling prior seasons to Netflix also allows studios to recoup their losses from shrinking DVD sales.

The final money-making opportunity comes by selling overseas rights: non-U.S. networks and MVPDs will buy rights to the shows, and a hit show can make a huge profit through these sorts of deals as there will be a new deal for each and every market. While it used to take American shows years to make the voyage overseas, the difference between U.S. and overseas launches can now be just days.

THE NETFLIX CONUNDRUM: One of the more clever moves Netflix has made has been to acquire full seasons of many recent hit TV shows. This was partly a visionary move and partly a reaction to the fact that Netflix's movie catalog was fairly light. Regardless, the studios rapidly became addicted to the millions of dollars Netflix was paying them for seasons two, three and four of their hits.

In addition to making the networks and studios quite rich, buying full seasons of popular series allowed for the rise of binge viewing. (More about that in the following section.) But as the MVPDs realized the strength of the market for full seasons, they began pressuring the studios to sell them full season VOD rights instead—especially for the current season (the "full in-season stack," in industry parlance). Which the studios were only too happy to do until Netflix told them that if they did so, they would no longer pay them countless millions for the older seasons, since those seasons would become less valuable. This was a problem because the studios had gotten very used to that income. But at the same time, they were aware that making all episodes of the current season available on the MVPDs VOD services would do more to increase current season tune-in, especially for new shows that were gradually building buzz. Hence the ongoing dilemma.

UNIONS: Like all other content producers, networks must negotiate deals with the powerful SAG/AFTRA (Screen Actors Guild/American Federation of Television and Radio Artists), WGA (Writers Guild of America—East and West) and DGA (Directors Guild of America) unions. Theses unions make sure their members are paid for the work they do, both the first time the show runs and from subsequent broadcasts, both in the U.S. and overseas. Deals with the unions are frequently part of the "rights issues" mentioned when people question why the TV industry can't do something, particularly something digital. The actors and writers and producers all (rightfully) want to get paid when their work runs on another medium and the contracts are structured to include this.

For the networks, this means that OTT broadcasts often include additional costs as OTT is considered to be a digital or internet broadcast. (This applies to commercials as well, which is part of the reason why networks can't run the same ad load on OTT as they do on their live broadcast—even when the OTT broadcast is an in-home live stream sent through the viewer's home WiFi network. More on that later too.)

PLAYER #4: THE PREMIUM NETWORKS

HBO, Showtime, Cinemax, Red Zone and other sports networks. These are the ad-free cable networks who started out showing movies but really made their mark by introducing high quality original content. Freed from the constraints of having to please advertisers, the premium networks were allowed to introduce more adult themes on their shows, both plot-wise and by allowing nudity. The quality of the shows helped usher in a second "golden age of television" and made these networks a must-have for many Americans, especially the affluent 25—54 demographic.

How Do They Make Money?
Subscriptions. The subscriptions are sold via the MVPDs who collect the money for them and keep a percentage for themselves as a profit. Subscriptions to the various premium networks are often bundled together, so that HBO makes money every time someone decides they want to watch the Showtime series *Homeland;* chances are good that the upgrade will consist of a premium channel bundle which gives the viewer access to both HBO and Showtime, along with Cinemax, Starz, and some smaller premium networks.

Not having to collect money from users every month is a huge plus for the premium networks, who also get to rely on the MVPD's marketing machines to promote their products. It's one of the main reasons why, despite frequent calls of many in the tech community, many actual industry observers were surprised in

October 2014 when HBO announced their decision to launch HBO Go as a standalone app. In addition to having to do their own marketing, they'd now have to set up billing, accounts payable, and customer service departments and deal with the attendant headaches of running those sorts of divisions. (Recent reports indicate the HBO plans to continue to outsource the aforementioned functions, this time to manufacturers of devices like Roku and Chromecasts and to the MVPDs as well, this time as part of a broadband package.)

Many observers (myself included) suspect that one of the main reasons HBO is introducing the standalone service is that it gives them an edge in negotiating their carriage deals with the MVPDs: give us what we want or we'll bolt and take our toys with us. That's a situation neither side wants to find themselves in, but so long as it's an option, it gives HBO the upper hand.

PLAYER #5: THE OTT SERVICES

Netflix, Hulu, Amazon, Vudu, iTunes, and all the other streaming services. (OTT = Over The Top, a reference to how web-based video is delivered—e.g. without a set-top box. Like MVPD, this is another industry term that's good to know.) Regardless of business model, they all started out as ways for consumers to watch the movie studios' back catalog and then quickly expanded into television where they serve the same function, giving viewers access to entire seasons of older series and enabling a behavior known as "binge viewing" where people plow through entire seasons of TV shows over the course of a few weeks, which makes for a very different experiences than watching 22 episodes weekly over the course of the year for five or six years.

How Do They Make Money?

Subscriptions (Netflix, Hulu, and Amazon Prime are known as SVOD services— Subscription Video On Demand). Viewers pay a set fee each month to watch an unlimited amount of content. Netflix maintains different pricing tiers based on the number of concurrent devices you want to be able to watch the service on, which helps cut down on the number of people sharing a single account.

Sales and Rentals (Amazon Instant Video, Vudu, iTunes, et al are known as TVOD service—Transactional Video On Demand). You can buy or rent a movie from the service. Rentals are far more popular than sales.

Subscription services have a slight edge here. They do not have the selection their counterparts have, especially in terms of new movies, but they have ease of use. Rentals are tough: rights issues limit the rental period to 48 hours and forbid renewals making it a tough sell. So is having to pay $3 or $4 every time you want to see a movie: with a monthly subscription, the viewer is less aware of the financial transaction.

ORIGINAL CONTENT: Like the premium cable services before them, the OTT networks have all set out to produce original content. Netflix has been particularly successful; its series *House of Cards* and *Orange Is The New Black* have both proved popular with critics and with audiences, based on the amount of buzz they receive. (Netflix does not release viewership numbers, so it's impossible to know exactly how many people are watching.) Amazon recently joined Netflix when the series *Transparent* won a Golden Globe award for best comedy.

NETWORK CONTENT: Netflix has twice stumbled onto exceptionally popular business models: first with streaming video, which no one had expected to take off as quickly as it did, and then by licensing full seasons of old TV shows. Here Netflix stumbled onto the fact that there was a large stockpile of quality TV shows, often shot on HD, that people wanted to watch but either hadn't jumped on the bandwagon at the beginning and now found themselves hopelessly behind, or they'd been too young when the series first aired. Regardless of why, binge-viewing took off like wildfire, and Netflix was the main beneficiary of that trend.

PLAYER #6: STREAMING DEVICES

Roku, Apple TV, Chromecast, and Amazon Fire are all small devices, either in the form of a "hockey puck" or a USB stick, that attach to the viewers' TV set and allow them to watch a range of OTT services directly on their TV.

How Do They Make Money?
Direct sales to consumers. Though Roku is moving into Pay-Per-View specials (think 1980s HBO), and they're all looking for licensing deals with TV manufacturers and MVPDs (similar to the ones Cablevision and TimeWarner inked with Roku this year.) The prospects for these devices is particularly strong in developing countries, where TV is likely to skip the cable-to-the-house phase.

It remains to be seen whether these devices will remain as standalones or if the TV set manufacturers will incorporate them into their systems. As noted previously, the difficulty of updating an $800 TV set versus a $50 Roku would seem to indicate that they will remain as separate devices.

BYOD: With the possible exception of Comcast, which is building out its own state-of-the-art set-top box, most MVPDs would be happy to see the traditional box disappear. They're expensive, they're difficult to upgrade, and they cost the MVPD several hundred dollars every time they need to roll a truck out to install or repair one. More troublesome still is the fact that installation isn't foolproof and so customers are left waiting for technicians to show up, venting their anger on social media and otherwise leaving the impression that the MVPD doesn't care. A switch to a BYOD (Bring Your Own Device) scenario, where subscribers would get access to an app on the streaming device of their choosing is a scenario MVPDs are increasingly bandying about. The only thing stopping them is the fact that many households still have old-fashioned cathode ray analog TVs which won't work with the streaming devices. We'll look more closely at the ramifications of a BYOD scenario in the next section.

PLAYER #7: SECOND SCREEN PLATFORMS

Twitter, Facebook and a host of unique applications that are designed to allow viewers to interact with each other around TV shows or to interact with the shows directly. The interaction is generally assumed to happen on a tablet or smartphone, hence the moniker "second screen."

How Do They Make Money?
Advertising seems to be the preferred model here, though the sale of and/or interpretation of data should also come into play.

While "second screen" is a great catch-all term, the range of interaction models (let alone business models) makes it difficult to issue grand pronouncements on the entire segment. Each piece currently has its strengths and weaknesses.

SOCIAL TV: While Twitter did an excellent job of convincing people outside of the TV industry that it plays a major role within the TV industry, the truth is not that settled: Twitter gets traction with live event shows, live sporting events and with a handful of scripted shows. But for most of the shows that are on TV, it's a non-entity. (Remember that Twitter is used by somewhere between 20 and 30 percent of the U.S. population. That leaves 70 or 80 percent of viewers out of the loop.) Additionally, Twitter is limited to live TV— there's not much point in tweeting about a show you're watching two days after it ran. So as time shifting becomes more and more of a factor, the impact of Twitter and similar media lessens.

Both Twitter and Facebook have the potential to become drivers for live (same day) tune-in, something the networks desperately need. That's something else we'll look at in more detail in the next section.

APPS: While there are many companion apps for TV shows, enabling everything from rating to commenting to sharing in the hopes of getting rewards, their biggest problem has been getting downloads and usage. No third-party app has broken away from the pack, and many observers are starting to wonder if the model of concurrent interaction is the problem: Do viewers really want to interact with each other or with the TV while they're watching television, and is an independent third-party app the way they want to conduct this interaction? So far the evidence seems to be telling us "no."

PLAYER #8: SMART TVS

Samsung, Sony, Panasonic and other manufacturers

How Do They Make Money?
Direct sales to consumers. The additional "smart" features are used to justify higher prices than "dumb" HDTVs, though as new features are introduced, the prices for older models tend to drop.

ADOPTION: While the advantage of a smart TV is the ability to use an app-like button built into the set's interface as an easy way to connect to Netflix or Facebook, several studies in the U.S. and U.K. show that many (if not most) consumers don't bother hooking up the smart TVs to the internet. Difficulty of set-up is the most likely reason for that, though the lack of demand for the smart TV's text-based apps (e.g. Facebook) also figures prominently

CRITICAL MASS: Perhaps the biggest challenge facing smart TV manufacturers is their inability to reach critical mass. To begin with, there's no interoperability between the various manufacturers. This is a problem in that the average American home has three TV sets and the odds of them all being LG or Samsung is fairly low. Americans also replace their TV sets around once every seven years. So the odds of someone throwing out all three TV sets and replacing them with smart TVs from a single manufacturer are even lower. Then there's the upgrade cycle: each new batch of models have features not found on previous models. That limits adoption to the subset of people who've bought that particular model which makes it hard to view smart TVs as anything other than a high priced experiment.

SUMMARY

Change Happens Gradually and Then All at Once. The TV industry is in the same place the cell phone industry was just before the introduction of the iPhone: all the pieces are there, it's just that no one's bothered to put them together.

There's no pressure on anyone to innovate because no one's disrupting the market in a major way (the way Napster once disrupted the music industry) and so there's no business reason to be an innovator; innovation is risky and most companies are risk-averse.

Eventually, someone will toss that bomb into the crowd and blow things up, the way the iPhone blew up the cell phone market. It may be Google or Apple or Intel or it may be a new start-up, someone you've never heard of.

Whoever it is, it has to be someone who feels their current market position is tenuous enough to make a risky move worth it. And what's important to remember is that right now there's no one in the TV industry who fits that description: profits are up, not down.

But it will happen, and once it happens, change will come quickly. And everything you've just read will be completely and hopelessly out-of-date.

SECTION 2

Change Is Coming Soon: What's Disrupting The Industry Today

THE REVOLUTION HAS BEGUN

The television revolution has begun, though it might not always seem that way, especially when you're looking at the program guide on your TV set and thinking how it looks like 1996, especially when you compare it to your smartphone or tablet.

Some of that is due to rights issues, some of it is because the industry has been slow to change, and some of it is because television has always had to accommodate the lowest common denominator and much of the audience is still not particularly tech savvy. Or, to put it another way, there are still lots of houses with old-school cathode ray TVs.

So what's stopping the revolution? It's not just older users with cathode ray TVs. It's TV networks and MVPDs who are unable, unwilling, or unready to adapt to the changes and figure out ways they can use these changes to make even more money. Mostly because they don't have to: there's no compelling business reason for them to change right now, because they're all still making money hand over fist. There are a lot of looming changes, but it's easy to see them all as far off. And so no one wants to go first, because, well, what if they're wrong?

Take the program guide. Why does Netflix have such a sexy-looking program guide while your MVPDs program guide looks like something from the Clinton administration? Rights issues. Networks pay for their place in the program guide. They want to be channel 2 or channel 4 (or whatever they were in the pre-cable days) and a more graphic guide would displace that. So the sexier, cooler guide is never the default. (At least not yet.) That's just one easy example of why the industry seems so far behind.

That said, the close to 50 million houses with Netflix are on the other end of the spectrum. They are at the forefront of the revolution, and Netflix is far from the only game in town. As we'll see in the next section, there are lots of changes afoot with a lot of obstacles still in the way.

The revolution has started. Now it's just a question of how it will play out.

TIME SHIFTING

For years, viewers watched television on a linear schedule, which meant that if you missed an episode of a series you were following, you had to wait for summer rerun season to catch it.

VHS recorders, which came on the scene in the 1980s, allowed viewers to record a show and watch it on their own schedule, skipping through commercials along the way. While initially popular, they were notoriously hard to program, the picture quality was less than ideal, and each tape only held a few hours of video, making the whole system more than a bit unwieldy.

In 2000, a new device called TiVo burst onto the scene, promising to completely revolutionize the way we watched TV. TiVo would record all your favorite shows for you, even suggesting (and recording) shows it thought you might like. The device was well reviewed and well received by the tech community, but failed to catch on with the general public.

Why that happened (or didn't happen, as the case may be) is still the subject of much debate (and something I'll get into in a later chapter), but TiVo was quickly elbowed aside by MVPD-supplied all-in-one set-top box/DVR units.

Unfortunately, those devices were clunky (to put it nicely) and many seemed to require an advanced engineering degree to figure out how to program them. As a result, DVR usage never really took off the way many had expected, and adoption rates in the U.S. stayed below 50 percent.

Despite these rocky beginnings, non-linear viewing, or "time shifting" has skyrocketed over the past few years, and its effects are currently rocking the industry to its core.

In December 2014, NBC research chief Alan Wurtzel confided that close to 40% of NBC's programming was watched on a time-shifted basis. That's a massive change in viewer behavior from ten years prior when close to 100% of viewing was live, and the change will affect everything from programming decisions to advertising rates.

What happened to cause this seismic shift? Several things. The popularity of non-linear streaming services like Netflix helped viewers grow accustomed to watching TV on their own schedules. At the same time, improved interfaces on both MVPD VOD (Video On Demand) systems and DVRs made those platforms easier to use, while the ability to watch TV on tablets and smartphones brought portability into the equation. Once viewers could watch whatever they wanted, wherever they wanted, then whenever wasn't far behind.

Time shifting has made a shambles of the ratings system, the linchpin of the business of television. Nielsen, the MVPDS, the networks and advertisers are all scrambling to find a way to make sense of a world where close to half of all viewers no longer watch live TV. The fallout is even more pervasive, and almost every one of the shifts we're currently seeing can somehow be tied back to the effects of time shifting. Take binge viewing, for instance, yet another trend that's currently altering the very nature of the television industry.

BINGE VIEWING

Binge viewing, the process of racing through en entire season (or seasons) of a show via streaming services like Netflix and Amazon, should have happened a lot sooner. We've had DVDs and DVRs for a while now, and iTunes has been carrying entire seasons of TV shows for many years.

So why now?

Part of the reason is psychological: streaming services like Netflix and HBO Go let viewers watch entire series without paying extra or downloading. It's the lack of commitment that gives people the permission they need to binge; somehow paying even $1.99 an episode felt like a commitment, felt like admitting you didn't have a whole lot else going on other than catching up on seasons 4 to 6 of *Lost*.

TV shows changed too. Production values for shows filmed over the past 10-15 years aren't appreciably worse than they are today. Most everything was shot in HD so the shows don't look dated the way shows from the 70s and 80s do. That means there's a whole lot more programming to binge on. If you're a teenager who was too young to have watched *Lost* when it was airing live, Netflix gives you an excellent way to watch the entire series—without having to ask your parents for the money to pay for it.

It's not just older American series that are fueling binge-viewing. Buzzworthy British shows like *Black Mirror*, *Peaky Blinders* and *Broadchurch* are available on Netflix and Amazon, and if the recent spate of "great British series to watch online" articles are any indication, it's become something of a badge of honor among the chattering classes to discover them before your friends do.

Additionally, the way TV shows were written has changed too. This happened around the time the DVR was introduced. Previously, shows were written so that a viewer who was watching the most recent episode for the first time would be able to catch up and immediately figure out what was going on. This prevented the creation of story arcs that stretched across a season or even several seasons. Once this barrier was removed (with the introduction of the DVR), writers were able to create shows that built on themselves, that required the viewer to have watched the show from the start. This development also encouraged binge viewing, as people who'd missed the first season or two of popular current shows were able to go back and catch up so they understood what was going on in real time.

So how popular is binge-viewing? A recent study I did at Piksel showed that over 90% of viewers had binge-watched at least one show, and the behavior showed no sign of abating. (Although it should be caveated that this figure was limited to a specific segment of the population, and that only about 50% of U.S. TV viewers own DVRs.)

People have compared binge viewing to reading a novel, and for certain types of shows, it is. Remember too that Dickens and other nineteenth-century authors released their books in serialized form, a new chapter a month. Reading all those chapters together as a novel is in many ways just like binge-viewing an entire series. There's continuity and the chance to view the work as a whole rather than as individual segments.

THE LILLYHAMMER EFFECT

Further fueling the trend to binge-viewing was what I call the "Lilyhammer Effect"—Netflix's decision to release all episodes of their original series at once. *Lilyhammer*, a comedy/drama starring ex-*Sopranos* cast member Steve Van Zandt as an American detective based in Norway, was first out of the box with this new format, and the decision proved popular enough that Netflix has continued it on all of their new original series, shows like *House of Cards*, *Arrested Development*, and *Orange Is The New Black*.

There had been much speculation around how Netflix would handle the release of their new original series, given the non-linear nature of the service: would they try and recreate the structures of linear TV, and, if so, how could they take time zones into account? Would they release the show at say 8PM for East Coast IP addresses and then wait three hours before releasing it for west coast ones? Would new episodes be released weekly, daily or in blocks of two or three at at time?

Netflix surprised many observers with their decision to release all episodes at once, thus giving viewers every incentive to binge watch.

The decision wasn't totally without precedent: research has shown this to be an excellent tactic for short-form content: viewers get hooked on a series by watching three or four episodes at once and don't have to remember to return to the site on a weekly basis.

Which is why Netflix's play was at once brilliant and revolutionary. Because suddenly the whole notion of linear TV was completely off the table and replaced by the sort of fully on demand line-up many futurists had been predicting.

The effects of this sort of shift will be myriad. Take the way TV shows are currently marketed, for instance. Rather than rely on on-air promos and growing buzz over the course of the season, TV shows will need to be marketed more like movies, with a huge build-up around the initial release date, followed by a combination of paid media and social buzz as follow-through. There will be a long tail for shows that enjoy popularity as reruns or as "cult classics," but for most shows, the initial release will be do-or-die time.

The "Lilyhammer Effect" will also have a major influence on how TV shows are developed. Currently, with a 22-episode season that plays out over six months, writers have the option of shifting the emphasis to a breakout minor character or dropping a plot line that seems unpopular with audiences. But with a whole season to deliver at once, writers will have to rely on instinct and luck.

Production schedules will feel the impact too. While network TV shows are currently written, filmed, and edited week by week, with writers and actors racing to keep up with constant deadlines, the new series will be able to be shot all at once. This may create some economies of scale, but will also demand a greater commitment from networks: they no longer have the option of shutting down an unpopular series after a few episodes. So look for shorter seasons, with producers putting out six or eight show seasons to both cut risk and lessen the time between seasons.

That's been the case for children's series and other non-prime time programming for years, notes Michele Band, who recently directed the series "Creative Currents" for Amazon. "The biggest difference will be in the editing," she says, "since you won't be able to adjust for audience reactions from week to week."

There may also be a push towards more dependent story lines, to push viewers to view another episode in order to find out what happens next. (Instant gratification is a huge motivator.)

If the all-at-once model is adopted by the networks, monetization will be a challenge as well, particularly with an ad-based model. Ads will need to be dynamically inserted as the viewer is watching, while taking time and place into account. But how do you prevent overexposure when a viewer is watching seven episodes of a series in one sitting? How is value calculated? These and other questions will need to be solved if a non-linear, binge-heavy viewing pattern becomes the norm.

Data will also come into play as networks will be better able to track viewing habits, understanding how many viewers drop off from episode to episode, who those viewers are and where they live. They'll be able to track the viewers' journey as well: how many episodes did they watch at once, how frequently do they watch them and in what order? The data from binge viewers will help networks to make better programming decisions, both creatively and from a monetization standpoint. But remember that Big Data is only starting to develop, and its role in the TV industry is still far from clear; data can be used to help make creative decisions, but many fear that data-based decisions cater to the lowest common denominator. Is big data the enemy of creativity? Truly breakthrough creative ideas rarely test well as the audience has never seen them before and needs time to adjust to them. The tension between these two ideals will continue for some time to come and there is no clear black-and-white answer: both sides have a point.

As more shows continue to be developed along this all-at-once model, consumers will have more choice than ever. But the question that remains unanswered is will they want that choice? Will they want to have to make active decisions every time they turn on the TV, or will they still prefer a system where someone else is making that choice? There are arguments to be made on both sides: better quality programming means better choices, but the type of TV-as-background-noise viewing so many people engage in weighs in favor of linear channels.

In the end it may be both—there's no reason there needs to be an either/or scenario. We'll look at possible scenarios in the next section.

SUMMARY

Binge-viewing is here to stay. A profusion of high-quality, well-produced series available online via streaming services is fueling this behavior. Younger viewers are using it to catch up on series that went off the air before they were old enough to appreciate them, breathing new life into old shows and everyone is using it to catch up on current hits they didn't watch from the beginning.

Binge viewing is also disrupting the production process as

entire seasons of a series are being released at once. This allows for a strong auteurial voice, but prevents writers from reacting to audience input as the season rolls out.

DISRUPTION POTENTIAL: 8

THE SHIFTING VALUE OF OWNERSHIP

One of the most significant changes happening today, something that affects every industry, not just television, is the shifting value of ownership. The idea of ownership is based on the concept of scarcity: if a certain good or service is scarce, it's of value to own it. But if it's plentiful, then ownership is of less value. Different cultures place different values on ownership. If you remember your American history, the Native Americans were often confused by the European notion of land ownership, land being open and plentiful on the Great Plains.

So too with music, TV, and movies these days: when they are available whenever and wherever you want them, the idea of consumer ownership seems pointless. This wasn't always the case however, and a quick look back can help us understand how we got to where we are today.

In 2007, the music industry was still reeling. The conventional wisdom of the day said that two things killed the music business. The first was piracy, in the form of Napster, Limelight, and other services that people used to download entire libraries of music that they could play on their computers and MP3 players. The second was the death of the album, which allegedly came at the hands of Apple.

The belief was that because iTunes let listeners cherry pick the songs they wanted to buy, people stopped buying albums, and because iTunes had a virtual lock on online music, Apple ignored the music industry's pleas to raise prices on downloads, which would have allowed them to recoup some portion of their shrinking profits.

Many people believed that it wasn't a question if these twin viruses would infect other industries, but when.

The conventional wisdom of the day also held that people wanted to own media. Owning movies was a habit that VHS and Betamax players helped start back in the 1970s, and people had been buying music for even longer. There was no reason to think that they would not continue to do so. Rental options existed, but their business models were based on the notion of limited supply which served to encourage sales rather than cannibalize them.

It was precisely because of this belief that the notion of digital lockers like UltraViolet took off. The idea was that the digital locker would prevent piracy, as people would not have physical access to all those digital files they owned, and that it would prevent any one company (i.e., Apple) from owning the digital marketplace and fixing prices. (It was widely held that consumers stuck with iPods because their considerable iTunes libraries did not work on other players. A digital locker with files that worked on any device, current or future, would ensure that did not happen again.)

It was a great idea in 2008, but then the market changed in a way that no one had predicted.

Sometime in the period between 2008 and 2012, consumers, or at least a significant number of them, started to accept the notion being promulgated by companies like Netflix and Spotify that they didn't really need to own music or movies; they were happy to lease them for a monthly subscription fee in exchange for unlimited access to a close-to-unlimited library.

Part of that decision had to do with the superior user experience of the subscription services. Unencumbered by fears of piracy and the need to keep track of individual libraries, they could keep their interfaces free from multiple log-ins and other protect-the-content features that digital lockers and similar services were forced to add.

But mostly it seemed to be a part of a gradual awakening by consumers to the fact that there was no longer a reason to own any sort of media. Storing everything in the cloud eliminated the notion of scarcity. It meant that everything would now be available to everyone. And you could watch or listen to it immediately for one low monthly fee.

We'd never had that before. Media was always scarce. Libraries only had so many copies of a given book. Owning media was the only way to ensure consistent access. But now there was a better way. One that gave you access to the entire spectrum of available content.

The value of ownership is fading on a macro level, particularly among the younger generation. Which is perhaps not surprising when you look at our recent history. For years, people owned very few things. Even rich people; the gilded-age mansions of Newport are not known for their lavish walk-in closets. And then, very quickly, the postwar consumer revolution of cheaply made goods turned ownership from novel to commonplace and suddenly we owned more things than we could keep track of. At which point ownership reached a tipping point and began to lose its value.

We can see that same change in the automobile industry: young people, who grew up in an era where owning two cars was fairly common, are buying fewer cars. And even the ones who own cars report that it's less of a big deal than it was a generation ago. Not all of them. Not most of them. But enough of them that automakers are noticing the shift, noticing the success of non-ownership options like ZipCar (a car-sharing service) and Uber (an app-based taxi service.)

That's how we got here. To a world where consumers would rather pay Netflix $9/month to be able to watch any show they want rather than pay the studio $35 for the right to own a boxed set of Season 2 of a particular series in perpetuity.

The future of media is in that change, in the triumph of convenience over quality, in the idea that there will always be a way to access any type of content at any time on any device. Those are the principles our future systems—and future business models—need to be based on. Consumers may not be aware that they've made this decision for us, but they have, and trying to buck that decision makes as much sense as trying to turn back time.

How that plays out as the TV industry moves forward will be interesting to watch. Movie studios still hold on to the hope that they can make the ownership model stick, but for television, the notion of selling $40 DVD sets seems to be a thing of the past. One option that may come into its own is the ability to pay to watch TV without commercials. It's an appealing idea for consumers, but maybe a tough sell for the networks, who are still afraid of alienating advertisers.

It's still an intriguing notion though. Television is the only medium where the ad-supported model is viewed as the preferred model. Mobile apps, for instance, use the opposite approach—the free version contains ads, but consumers who like the app can pay for the premium ad-free version.

I've often wondered how this model would work on TV. In summer 2013, for instance, CBS produced a mini-series based on the Stephen King novel "Under The Dome." It ran on CBS on Monday nights (with commercials) and then on Amazon on Friday nights without commercials. It would have seemed to make more sense to swap that arrangement and have had the commercial-free Amazon version run first, even charging fans extra for this premium experience. That would have allowed fans of Stephen King's story to sign up in advance and serve as evangelists for the ad-supported version, which would then be the standard (or sub-premium) experience.

When I ran this notion by several people from the networks and ad-buying services they had a similar reaction: advertisers would not be happy about this as they'd regard it as an admission by the networks that they perceived the ads that supported their content as undesirable. An odd notion for consumers who rarely see commercials as anything but undesirable, but for advertisers paying millions of dollars for a single spot, it's a perfectly logical argument.

And in that argument we can see the crux of the issues facing the industry and preventing it from moving forward at a more rapid pace: what seems perfectly obvious to the people watching the shows is not always obvious to the people creating and/or paying for them. In order for things to progress, both sides have to be aligned. Whether or not that will happen and in enough time to make a difference are two key questions that remain to be answered.

Only time will tell.

SUMMARY

In a world where media is always available, the value of ownership has dropped tremendously.

Viewers are happy to instantly stream the shows they want whenever they want and no longer see the value of owning a DVD or a digital copy of a movie when they can just as easily stream it.

DISRUPTION POTENTIAL: 7.5

VIDEO ON DEMAND (VOD)

VOD, or video on demand, has long been the red-headed stepchild of the industry. It was originally designed to be a marketing tool: viewers would see all the shows available on VOD and be impressed with the depth and breadth of each network's offerings and, by extension, the MVPDs. The worst-case scenario was that they'd watch a few episodes before deciding to watch it live. Why worst case? Because VOD didn't have commercials. So a viewer watching shows via VOD was a viewer who wasn't making anyone any ad revenue.

That attitude is also why the VOD menus on most MVPDs are such wet hot messes. Not only are they difficult to find (Time Warner's, for example, is on a random channel) and difficult to navigate, they often use confusing nomenclature: my FIOS system, for example, features "Popular Shows" and "Hit Shows" as two of the top-level options—it's up to you to figure out which category the program you're looking for falls under, and what the difference might be. And then you've got to make sure you navigate correctly between the SD and HD versions. But again, the idea was never to make VOD a popular destination. Which is why most every network contract with the MVPDs only allows them to show the five or six most recent episodes of any given show—no one was thinking binge viewing was going to be a thing when these contracts were negotiated.

That's starting to change now. The MVPDs are beginning to

negotiate for the rights to show the entire current season (the "full in-season stack"), not just the most recent five episodes. (This is not going over very well with Netflix, which feels that giving the MVPDs rights to the full in-season stack undercuts the value of their second- and third-season rights.)

But as viewing habits are changing, the networks are realizing that viewers want to be able to watch what they want when they want. Which usually means choosing between one of two options: VOD or DVR. And since DVR means "users skipping commercials" the networks and MVPDs are beginning to see the beauty of VOD. Particularly VOD with commercials you can't fast-forward through, otherwise known as non-skippable VOD. This allows them to reap some advertising revenue without losing viewers to DVRs where their habits are less easily monetized.

The tortured interfaces described above are doing their part to keep VOD from becoming more widely adopted. Part of the blame for their existence comes from the deals the MVPDs have struck with the networks as to how the VOD content will be displayed, what categories it will be listed in, and what metatags the networks will provide. These deals, no doubt, sounded good on paper, but when they're up there on the screen, they only serve to confuse and frustrate viewers, contra to their original intent.

There's also the whole HD versus SD mess to contend with: so long as a number of viewers don't have HD TV's, VOD will have to be available in both formats, which makes the existing interfaces even more labyrinthine.

At the same time, networks are launching their own apps and websites where the same shows that play on VOD are available online. These apps often come with their own set of issues (viewers must authenticate by providing their MVPD's log-in information, something they rarely know and don't have an easy way to find). But they are easier to access once you're finally authenticated and the networks are able to better track the activity on them.

Netflix, Amazon, and (especially) Hulu are also competing for eyeballs with the MVPD's VOD offerings. Given how much more user-friendly their interfaces are and how easy it is to find exactly what you're looking for, viewers don't have much incentive to try the MVPD's VOD offerings, and now that they've had a few years to get comfortable with Netflix and its kin, it is going to be harder than ever to lure them back.

And while the MVPDs were remiss in not seeing the revolution coming, the truth is, hardly anyone did. The one lesson we've learned from the digital age is that convenience trumps quality: the music industry did not think anyone would listen to MP3s because the quality was so poor compared to CDs and vinyl. The phone companies did not think people would use rectangular cell phones they couldn't cradle between their shoulders and necks for hours. The movie industry didn't think people would put up with the buffering on streaming services (forgetting how frequently rental DVDs skipped, got stuck, and otherwise acted like prima donnas).

They were wrong. People prefer convenience, and Netflix, Hulu, and Amazon offer it to them in spades.

The final piece of the VOD puzzle is full-length movies. The MVPDs have begun realizing that they have larger movie catalogs than Netflix and, more importantly, they have the newest releases. Here again, the problem is the interface: while Netflix, Amazon and Vudu have well-laid-out, intuitive, easy-to-search interfaces, the typical MVPD interface is anything but. Here there are no networks to blame, but the MVPDs haven't stepped up their game on their movie catalogs because they fear that a well-designed VOD store will compete with their own TV content, pulling viewers away from network TV.

This is probably not true. In all likelihood the viewer will find the on-demand movies on Amazon, iTunes, Vudu, or a host of other OTT movie services. They've set out to watch a movie and they realize that there are options beyond their MVPD's VOD store. Which means many of them don't even bother to look there at all. The MVPDs are starting to react though, slowly but surely giving some attention to their movie catalogs and promoting them to their customers as an alternative to OTT services.

As VOD has become more popular and more a part of the landscape, the networks and MVPDs have discovered the value of non-skippable VOD and more and more of them are making it a default feature, especially for recent network shows. As networks and studios accept the inevitability that a sizable portion of their audience will want to watch on their own schedule (i.e., time-shifting), VOD may become more ubiquitous and every show may be available on demand.

In Europe, we've already seen the rise of "catch-up TV"—a feature where, if you come into a live program, say, 15 minutes late, you're able to start watching from the beginning. This isn't readily available in the U.S. (Time Warner is one of the only MVPDs that offers it), which has more to do with rights issues (catch-up shows need to be recorded somewhere so they can be played back), but eventually this too may be seen as a must-have, rather than a nice-to-have.

So if it's adopted across the board, a default system of making every show available on VOD with non-skippable commercials may well be the savior for the TV industry's current ad-supported model, something we'll discuss in more detail in the next section.

SUMMARY

As just about every show will be available via VOD once it's aired, the percentage of TV that's viewed in a linear fashion will drop precipitously.

MVPDs will offer non-skippable VOD (VOD with embedded dynamically inserted commercials you can't skip) as a way to retain ad revenue.

DISRUPTION POTENTIAL: 9.5

STREAMING VIDEO PLATFORMS

The sudden and overwhelming success of Netflix's streaming service took the entire industry by surprise, including, it's been said, its CEO, Reed Hastings. Internet video had, for so many years, been a slow, laborious project, subject to endless buffering, crashing files, pixelated frames, and worse. So what made Netflix, the darling of mail-order DVDs, think that their system was going to actually take off?

Part of the answer comes from this simple experiment: Take an old DVD. One that may not always have been carefully stored in its jewel case and held exclusively from the sides. Put it in your DVD player. Now watch how many times the DVD skips, freezes, and crashes.

And there you have your answer. Streaming movies in 2009 wasn't necessarily a seamless experience. But it was no worse than watching the well-worn DVDs you got from Netflix and Blockbuster. And there was the promise that streaming would soon get better, that bandwidths were improving every day.

The key benefit of streaming, however, was the fact that it was instant. Movies had been available for download for a while, but internet speeds were slow, movies were big files, and downloading a movie from iTunes took well over a half hour, meaning that you probably could have gotten in your car, driven down to Blockbuster, come back, microwaved some popcorn and been ten minutes into the movie in the same time it took to download a movie to your hard drive.

Which was another issue: movie files took up space while streaming files didn't. People didn't want to trash their movie files, especially if they owned them, but they took up a lot of room on the hard drive, and without a regular clean-up to move them to an external drive, they could quickly overwhelm your laptop. Streaming let you avoid that problem because the only things that needed to be saved were some temporary buffers.

Which leads us to the most significant disruption streaming video has enabled: suddenly consumers have access to vast catalogs of movies and TV shows, whenever and (more or less) wherever they want them. Rather than being tied to the linear stream or the size of their hard drive, they're able to choose from thousands of titles, and they're able to do so on their own schedules. That's a huge disruption.

Streaming also enabled portability, particularly within the home. If you had WiFi in your house you were able to move your laptop into the bedroom, out onto the deck, even into the bathroom, bringing video to places it had never been before. Cross-screen portability, the ability to stop watching on one screen and then pick up in that exact same spot on another was a well-marketed promise that really did offer a sea change to consumers, whose only prior option was linear video. It wasn't so much that they were moving from device to device, it was that they were able to have a place to watch video in just about every room in the house.

The final stretch for streaming video will be when mobile is a viable delivery system. Right now it's possible via a solid 4G/LTE connection, but reception is still so spotty in much of the U.S., that it's a non-issue. But as the number of WiFi and mobile towers grows and reception improves, viewers who want to watch out of the home (on a bus or a train, in a car, in the park, etc.) will be able to do so, and that will open up yet another option: the ability to watch video content out of home.

It's a option that I'm still somewhat skeptical about, because outside of live sports, weather, and news, there's not a huge demand for out of home viewing. No one is heading down to Starbucks to watch the latest episode of *Game of Thrones.* So while the ability to watch out of home will become available shortly, the number of actual use cases remains small, making it a nice-to-have feature rather than a must-have one. If you're a frequent business traveler, being able to access your own content from your hotel room is a nice perk, but the number of people who fit that use case doesn't constitute a profitable market segment. On the other hand, it's possible that once it's available, it could become a trend, especially given the shift to personal subscription services: if you are at a friend's house and you want to watch a show you've bookmarked, you might just use your service to connect (provided you can remember your password).

The final disruption caused by streaming is the huge amount of bandwidth it eats up. Studies showed that as early as 2012, something like 33% of all prime-time bandwidth in the U.S. was being used by Netflix.

That's in large part why the debate over net neutrality has taken off: Netflix is at the crux of the issue over whether it's fair to allow the MVPDs to provide dedicated lanes for specific video content. We'll discuss the overall ramifications of net neutrality in the next chapter, but the vast amount of bandwidth streaming video eats up has other implications as well.

Take overall bandwidth speeds, for instance. Since streaming has become popular, MVPDs have worked to increase their bandwidth speeds, particularly as Google entered the market with its Google Fiber service which provided speeds of 1G. Netflix pushed the market along some too by publishing monthly reports on which MVPD systems were best at streaming Netflix content, a report that basically became a free ad for the top providers and a great sales tool for them as well. The result has been higher bandwidth across the board and a realization that greater speeds are still needed as 4K and 8K transmissions are on the horizon. 4K is the next step after HD, providing sharper picture quality and greater detail. Netflix has already announced that they plan to start shooting all their shows in 4K, and other studios are sure to follow suit. As consumers replace their current HDTVs with 4K ones, they're going to want to watch 4K shows and movies, and the speeds to allow that will have to follow, pushing bandwidth speeds even higher.

QAM vs Streaming: Cable television signals have traditionally been delivered via a technology solution known as QAM (quadrature amplitude modulation.) It's not necessary to understand exactly how QAM works, but suffice it to say it was able to deliver a very crisp picture. The knock on video delivered via the internet, known as IPTV (for dedicated streams) and OTT (for streams on the open internet), was that the quality was not nearly as good as QAM and that consumers would never go for it.

If that sounds familiar, it's because it's similar to the argument the music industry made about MP3s: they didn't sound as good as CDs or vinyl, and thus consumers would never adopt them en masse. Only that wasn't the case and consumers chose the convenience of MP3s over a difference in quality few seemed to notice. The same thing is happening now with video, as consumers choose the convenience of streaming and don't seem to be aware of any decline in picture quality.

SUMMARY

Streaming video is disrupting the industry in several ways.

Access: With streaming, viewers have instant access to vast catalogs of content that they can watch on their own schedules.

Place: Streaming video can be watched on a variety of devices (laptops, tablets, phones, streaming set-top boxes) anywhere there's an internet connection

Greater Bandwidth: In order to accommodate the vast amount of bandwidth video takes up, MVPDs have been forced to increase the amount of bandwidth they offer consumers.

DISRUPTION POTENTIAL: 9.0

NET NEUTRALITY

Net Neutrality is a much talked about but poorly understood theory about how to manage traffic on the internet. The basic notion is that no one should be forced to pay to have a functional pipeline for their content—i.e. no company should be able to pay for preferential treatment or access to bandwidth.

There's not a whole lot of pushback on the high-level part of the theory, which serves to protect smaller companies and start-ups and encourages innovation. Where Net Neutrality gets tricky, however, is in defining what exactly "equal access" entails.

Recent decisions by the FCC to allow for "internet fast lanes" have gotten many advocates in an uproar. But that's due more to a lack of understanding about how the internet actually works than it is a valid disagreement.

The cables that bring the internet to your home also bring television and television signals. Right now, those transmissions are usually done via analog technology on dedicated portions of the greater pipe. The MVPDs sell access to those dedicated portions to television networks as part of their carriage fee agreements. (e.g. "We TNT, agree to pay you, Comcast, X dollars, and as part of that, you will make sure that TNT broadcasts show up in people's houses looking good.") These agreements form the basis of every pay-TV arrangement.

Now as those networks switch from analog to digital, the digital signals will be traveling along those same dedicated spectra, but as digital signals, not analog and so the portion of the entire cable dedicated to digital internet signals becomes bigger. And it's the decision of the FCC to allow the MVPDs to determine how much of their overall bandwidth they want to give over to internet services (versus analog television and telephone)

As BTIG's Rich Greenfield, a noted Wall Street analyst points out "open Internet freedom fighters make it sound like the bandwidth/spectrum allocated to the Internet is fixed and anytime a fast lane is created, the rest of the Internet slows down. This is simply false."

To Greenfield's point, the internet is not a finite thing. So selling access to a dedicated "fast lane" doesn't de facto create slow lanes. At least not yet. The test will come when (and if) consumers do notice the difference, do notice that certain sites and channels seem considerably slower and less stable than their main competitors and when that differentiation starts to affect their ability to grow and maintain their subscriber base. That's a long time coming, if indeed it ever comes at all, and so for now it's not an issue.

In addition, net neutrality, as analyst Dan Rayburn frequently points out, "is an incredibly complex set of problems that people keep trying to simplify and politicians try to turn into sound bytes."

It's not as if Netflix uploads their files directly to Comcast, which then delivers it directly to your home. There are multiple parties involved, companies known as CDNs, or Content Distribution Networks, who take the files from the Netflixes of the world and deliver them to transit providers like Cogent, which then deliver them to the MVPDs, which serve as "last mile providers"—bringing the files from the internet to the consumers homes. Recent FCC rulings on net neutrality affect the MVPDs, but creation of fast and slow lanes is more likely to happen with transit providers or CDNs who operate out of public view.

MONOPOLIES AND DUOPOLIES

Net Neutrality gets especially tricky due to the fact that in the U.S., broadband internet is a monopoly—or in areas where AT&T Uverse or Verizon FIOS are available, a duopoly. That's it. There's very little competition, which leads to worries that a company could easily be shut out from the internet if the MVPDs don't like their content or, as we'll see in the next chapter, have a vested interest in ensuring a lack of success.

And that's a real issue because right now there is no realistic alternative to the major broadband providers. It's why so many "death of television" manifestos end up claiming that people are going to give up their Comcast and FIOS broadband... for free WiFi at Starbucks. Because that's currently about it for alternatives: free WiFi at Starbucks or the free public WiFi that some cities now offer in limited locations. And if you've ever tried to watch even a 30-second YouTube video on free WiFi, you'll know why that's not really an option.

So what is?

Well, here's where things get complicated. Because right now, the only realistic possibility for change is going to come courtesy of the United States government, which has it within its power (either Congress, the courts or the FCC) to break the stranglehold the MVPDs have on broadband and unbundle those "last mile" connections.

If this ever happens it's not going to be because so many people are pissed off about having to pay for 800 channels they never watch or because they can't watch the Olympics online or because they have to use their parents' log-in to watch HBO. It's going to happen because the companies the French have nicknamed "GAFA" (Google, Apple, Facebook, and Amazon) have launched a major lobbying effort to make it happen.

Who stands to gain the most from the breakup of the television industry? GAFA. And who keeps getting punted every time they try to join the Television Industrial Complex? GAFA. Which is why I've been hearing rumors about how they've come to the conclusion (individually or together) that legislation is the only thing that's going to work. Because they've tried all the obvious routes: GAFA have all come to Hollywood, waving their billions, only to get rejected as they were shown deals that were too expensive to be profitable or not happening at all. Partly because the entertainment industry thinks of them as the scorpion in Aesop's The Frog and the Scorpion fable, but mostly because there's no compelling reason to give them a good deal. As Intel recently learned the hard way, without their own broadband connection, there's not much they can really offer in return.

And it's not like they haven't tried that angle either: Google is building out something called Google Fiber, a high-speed (1G) broadband and pay-TV service. But they launched that service around two years ago, and thus far they've wired up Kansas City, with nascent forays into Austin, Texas, and a few other small cities. It's a big country and laying your own cable isn't really a viable option—just ask FIOS: after spending billions to bring fiber optic cable to what essentially amounted to the upscale suburbs of the Northeast and parts of Los Angeels, they announced in 2010 that they were giving up on building out new territories and opting instead to fill in their existing territories.

Which leaves the federal government as GAFA's only viable option. GAFA needs an angle, of course, because stamping their collective feet and shouting "it's not fair!" is only going to get them so far. And it seems they've found that angle too, by claiming that the broadband monopolies leave Net Neutrality at the mercy of a single company.

GAFA will claim that by creating an oligopoly where access to broadband is controlled by one or two major carriers in any given market, we've created a situation where Net Neutrality is too easily compromised and thus we need to break open the system the way we once broke open Ma Bell.

The MVPDs, on the other hand, have a very compelling counterargument centered around the billions of dollars they've invested in building and maintaining that infrastructure and the inherent unfairness of a government deciding to take that all away from them.

While both sides have extremely deep pockets with which to lobby Congress, the MVPDs generally wind up dominating the list of America's most hated companies while GAFA are still pretty popular—a fact that should be keeping the former up at night.

What happens if GAFA wins and they get to have their own broadband pipes and the ability to set up their own pay TV services? Well that's when the TV industry should start to see a shake-up.

Maybe.

On the one hand, competition is the lifeblood of innovation, and the entrance of several well-liked, well-funded competitors should serve to shake things up and induce real changes in an industry that desperately needs them.

On the other, there's the fact that we still only have one source for popular, high-production value programming and the networks and studios are not going to roll over and accede to deals that negatively affect their bottom lines. Nor should they: they are businesses, not charities. So the sweeping changes may happen in slow waves, rather than all at once. (Factor in too the long-term deals and rights agreements already in place: those can't be trashed unless both parties agree to it.)

Nothing is a given however, especially government intervention. Which may take on many forms, including a push to build out a high-bandwidth free national WiFi network or to beef up municipal WiFi networks, since everyone seems to be in agreement that free, pervasive WiFi is a laudable goal. (It's on the matter of paying for it where people part ways.)

What's significant, though, is that both Washington and the mainstream media seem to be waking up to the fact that broadband has become a monopoly, and that this is not a good thing for anyone.

If change is going to come to the TV industry, it will come in the form of a shake-up to our current broadband infrastructure, as closed markets have no incentive to innovate, whereas open markets breed innovation. Only time will tell.

SUMMARY

Dedicated high-speed lanes are less of a threat to the industry than some onlookers would have you believe. There is nothing finite about the internet, and adding in dedicated fast lanes does not mean everyone else is in the slow lane. The focus on Net Neutrality has made the powers that be aware that broadband is a monopoly in most communities and this has a negative effect on both consumers and content producers. Therefore, there's a chance that the government (judiciary or

legislative branches) will break up the current MVPD line-up the way they once did to Ma Bell back in the 80s.

DISRUPTION POTENTIAL: 6.5

V-POPS

The advent of V-POPs (virtual pay-TV operators), a term coined by Colin Dixon of nScreen Media, has been heralded for quite some time now. The term refers to a traditional pay TV service that is delivered exclusively over the open internet.

It's something the existing MVPDs had been circling around for some time, but it was Dish, (whose CEO Charlie Ergen is known for his bold moves) that launched first, announcing their new Sling TV service in January 2015, a few steps ahead of Sony, whose Vue service was rolled out in March 2015.

The key to understanding V-POPs is that they won't be immediate hits: 90% of the U.S. already has pay TV, and it's unlikely that people will give up their existing service en masse in favor of a V-POP. That leaves new subscribers— e.g., cord nevers—who number in the hundreds of thousands, not millions. So regardless of how well received the service is, it will take a while before it takes off.

That's why the new Sling makes so much sense for Dish. It allows them to test out the notion of much smaller "skinny" bundles, something the MVPDs would love to be able to sell, as there is much demand for them; in addition to the basic $20 service, there are add-on packs, priced at $5 each, for news, sports and children's programming.

But Dish's decision to go with a smaller, low-priced package to attract millennial cord-nevers is what's interesting here. Most previous attempts at V-POPs were intended to be high-end products aimed at upscale consumers who wanted to replace their current system with something very stylish and easy to use. Dish took the opposite approach and went with a product aimed at people who'd never subscribed to pay TV before, offering them something that looked and felt an awful lot like Aereo, the web-only live broadcast TV service that the Supreme Court declared illegal last year. With fewer than 50 channels, it stands in marked difference to the 1000+ channels offered in most pay-TV packages.

That approach may or may not backfire on them: the presence of a full load of commercials seems to be the number-one slam on Sling for now (Vue and others face the same criticism), and for a cord never who's used to watching Netflix and other commercial-free services, it just might prove to be a deal breaker. Since all other V-POPs will also have to run with a full commercial load, it will be interesting to see what the reaction is to Sling. The industry has yet to fully acknowledge the degree to which services like Netflix and HBO Go are training consumers to watch TV without commercials and how much that's going to affect future behavior.

Sling, which (as the name implies) makes use of the Slingbox technology that Dish owns, is a $20/month package that gives viewers access to CNN, ESPN and a number of other stations including the Disney Channel and AMC.

What's notable here is that none of the major broadcast networks are included. Not because Dish doesn't see their appeal—it's just that securing the rights was impossible, too expensive, or both. (The fact that Nielsen would not be counting views on Sling most likely factored into their decision as well.)

The allure of a V-POP for Dish is that it allows them to reach a whole new set of customers, drawing them into the fold where they can be upsold and upgraded as the years go by.

That's why Sling's launch without either VOD or DVR capabilities is such a head-scratcher. Which is not to say these won't be rolled out shortly: Sling has been very good about adding channels to the line-up and the DVR and VOD capabilities may be under negotiation. What will be interesting to see, if they do launch is how much they'll enable viewers to avoid commercials. Will the DVR come with a 30-second skip button the way many MVPD remotes currently do? Will the VOD come with non-skippable ads built in, or will it be commercial-free?

And while those are interesting questions, what really remains to be seen is how much a live TV connection is worth to millennial viewers. Will the $20 a month Sling is charging seem like the right price to get access to both CNN and ESPN? Or will the intended audience decide it's too much money for a service they use fairly infrequently, mostly to catch the occasional football game or breaking news story?

Sling signed up 100,000 viewers in its first month, a number Dish says they are very happy with, but let's wait and see what that number looks like three and then six months out.

Sony's Vue service approaches the problem from the opposite angle: Sony has inked deals with Viacom and three of the big four networks (ABC is missing) and has a line-up of around 50 or so smaller channels as well (no unbundling there). Unlike Sling, Vue has a virtual DVR and all channels come with pause and rewind capability. The service costs between $50 and $70/month, depending on the package.

Vue's Achilles' heel seems to be that it only works on Playstation 3 and 4, which limits its audience to PlayStation's existing base, which is sizable, but still fairly limited.

If Dish wants to lure in more subscribers and Sony wants to sell more Playstations, what's in it for the terrestrial MVPDs?

That's a question many have been asking as it seems that Verizon may be getting ready to enter the fray, having recently acquired Intel's OnCue system.

OnCue was a noble experiment by Intel. Lead by Erik Huggers, who'd previously been Director of BBC's Future Media & Technology, where he was responsible for the BBC's Online, iPlayer, Mobile and Red Button services, Huggers' mission was to build Intel's own V-POP, which would be based around a piece of hardware, a proprietary set-top box. People who have seen the prototype in action have reported that it was for the most part very well designed and thought out.

So what went wrong? It was mostly Intel's inability to secure rights deals with most of the major U.S. networks that did them in. The networks either refused to play ball at all or they asked for incredibly steep carriage fees. Their rationale? The Intel service would only serve to antagonize their existing MVPD customers, undercutting their bargaining power with the Comcasts and Charters. Adding fuel to the fire was the fact that it did not appear to have a very good chance of survival.

The latter point was something many in the industry observed as well: Intel was asking a lot from consumers. It wanted them to place their faith in a company that had little to no experience in the television industry. It wanted them to give up their existing pay TV service and get rid of all their set-top boxes for a service that was being billed as a premium experience and would likely cost them more than they were currently paying.

Intel's new CEO, Brian Krzanich, was not a fan of the project, which had been championed by his predecessor Paul Otellini, and did not want Intel to get into the content game. And so in January of 2014, OnCue was sold to Verizon for considerably less than the $500 million the chip maker originally wanted. (Most estimates were for under $200 million)

Verizon hired Huggers and most of the 350 employees he'd collected but a full year later there are only intermittent rumors as to the service's imminent deployment as a mobile service, and Huggers parted ways with Verizon in May 2014 amid rumors that the company was no longer pursuing a V-POP strategy.

Recent rumors, however, imply that Verizon is looking to launch its service via its Verizon Wireless platform. That would give the company over 100 million potential subscribers throughout the country, but it also raises a new set of issues, namely how will the new service work? Will users only be able to access it via 4G wireless service or will they be able to use WiFi, and if it's 4G only, what about bandwidth caps? (Video eats up an awful lot of data.) And if they can't use WiFi, how will they get it on their TV?

Those same questions apply to Apple's long awaited Apple TV, which, according to a March 2015 article in the *Wall Street Journal* is going to come out this June, as a Sling-like "skinny bundle" priced somewhere between $30 and $40 per month.

Apple has yet to confirm or deny this rumor, though Apple TV may well exist by the time you read this book.

That said, the launch of other VPOPs does signal to consumers that the TV Industrial Complex is willing to grow and change. Something many did not think possible. What remains to be seen is if it's actually changed enough and if millennials will adopt the new V-POPs.

SUMMARY

While there has long been talk of someone launching an internet-only pay TV service or V-POP (virtual pay-TV operator), Dish was the first out of the gate with its Sling TV product, which was launched in January 2015. Sling features a limited line-up headlined by CNN and ESPN for just $20/month. They are pitching the product at cord-nevers who would like to have live news and sports coverage.

The initial market for V-POPs is not expected to be huge, but there is huge potential for it to grow, particularly among young people who currently don't have pay TV service. That said, the TVE apps the MVPDs offer have many advantages over the V-POPs and are in good position to become the default OTT platform of the future.

DISRUPTION POTENTIAL: 6.5

TABLETS AND SMARTPHONES

In 2005 I decided I wanted to catch up on the first two seasons of *Lost*, and so I downloaded and watched all 40-some-odd episodes on my iPhone. Once I'd figured out how to prop the phone up on a Rube Goldberg-esque pile of pillows in front of me, it was actually an okay experience, provided I didn't make any sudden moves to send the pile of pillows plummeting.

I wasn't alone either. A surprising number of people were also watching TV on their phones. They were joined by millions more when the iPad and other tablets came out. (There are all sorts of mildly conflicting statistics on the exact numbers, but to give some perspective, in a 2013 study, 23% of Netflix subscribers reported they'd watched TV on their smartphones, with 15% having watched on iPads. Bear in mind that stat itself is affected by the fact that many more people own smartphones than own iPads.)

ITunes was the earliest version of mobile television, and in its earliest iteration, viewers could only purchase downloads from the service. It took until September 2010 for Apple to secure the rights that allowed them to rent TV shows.

When Netflix launched their streaming service in 2009, it was still primarily viewed as a movie-watching service. And for a lot of Netflix users, the iPad was a great place to watch a movie. The touchscreen interface was a step up from clunky onscreen menus, and the iPad screen was a good size for individual viewing.

Still, it was Netflix's shift to TV shows that really pushed adoption of mobile devices as alternative screens. This had as much to do with volume—there are far more episodes of TV shows than movies—as it did with the fact that it's just easier to watch a half hour show on a hand-held device than it is a three hour movie.

The shift was particularly significant with teens and 20-somethings, the coveted millennial group, as they were already quite used to watching YouTube and other short form videos on their mobile devices. This helped fuel the myth that millennials exclusively watched TV on their devices.

In fact, it now seems like just about every conference I speak at features someone putting out the "teens prefer to watch TV on their iPads" myth, and I just wanted to set the record straight.

Teens (like adults) prefer to watch TV on the best and largest screen available—which, if you are an American teenager in 2015, is often your iPad: Mom and Dad are probably watching the big screen TV, and even if they aren't, they're in a position to comment on your viewing habits, which makes the relatively private iPad a better option.

Now one reason behind this dynamic may be the fact that many parents seem to have banished TVs from the bedroom, a result, no doubt, of the many articles outlining how harmful that was. (That, and there's no room anymore, between the laptop and the iPad.) That leaves the family-room TV as the only option, and if it's already occupied, then the tablet or laptop makes a good back-up.

There's also privacy: I firmly believe that the sexualization of American television, especially prime-time television, has contributed to teens wanting to watch TV away from their parents. Because if you're a 14-year-old, the last thing in the world you want to do is watch two characters going at it on TV, with arms, legs, thrusts, and moans while your Mom sits on the couch next to you. And since that's pretty much a given on almost any prime-time show, you turn to headphones and the iPad. (There's a comedian who has a routine about watching TV with his teenage daughter. He selected *Storage Wars* figuring it was relatively harmless. Only the episode turned out to be about storing sex toys, at which point he says that he and his daughter sat on the couch in silence, each trying to pretend the other wasn't there.)

Privacy aside, there's also the fact that high-production value

TV just looks better on a big HD screen. (And it will look even better still on the new 4K and 8K screens.) So if it seems that kids are avoiding the big screen in favor of their devices, it's only because someone else got there first.

"As much as there is a clear trend and shift toward the "instant gratification" offered via Video On Demand and streaming services to watch "catch up" TV, the massive bulk of U.S. audiences are still watching the majority of their TV the old-fashioned way: live—and on a TV set," noted Jeremy Toeman, senior vice president at Viggle. "It's clear that the future of TV watching will include more hybrid experiences, with some content we choose to watch anytime/anywhere, but that's unlikely to permanently replace the big screen/living room experience for the majority of Americans."

High production value (or higher production value, to be exact) is also driving viewing habits in the other direction: as the quality and bit rate of YouTube and other short-form video improves, the videos (which, not that long ago, looked sketchy even on an iPhone) are making the move to the big screen.

Devices like Chromecast and Amazon Fire and Roku allow users to quickly send YouTube video from their phones and tablets to their TVs where they actually look good, even on large screen HD sets. As this behavior has increased, there's been a realization that viewers still prefer a lean back experience and having to decide what to watch next every 90 seconds provides a suboptimal experience. That's why the idea of introducing playlists for short-form video based on user preferences has caught on. "We are all familiar with the comfort food feeling of sitting back on our couch and turning on the TV," notes Field Garthwaite, CEO of Iris, which creates a Pandora-like linear experience out of short form videos. "That feeling is the reason why we built Iris—because it is so difficult to recreate that experience on a phone or a laptop, and even harder to monetize it."

SUMMARY

While they probably won't replace the big screen TV in most

homes, smartphones and tablets do provide an alternate viewing location, one that's more private, personalized, and portable. That makes them a gold mine in terms of data, as it provides information about individual users across a range of screens. For the consumer, the benefit is in being able to have a personal video player with access to a wide range of content. While most smartphone viewing still consists of "snacking" (e.g., viewing short-form content) the ability to catch up on long-form content via TV Everywhere systems is a big plus for both programmers and audiences.

DISRUPTION POTENTIAL: 7.5

STREAMING DEVICES: THE NEW SET TOP BOXES

In September 2010, Apple introduced the second generation of Apple TV, a $99 device that allowed users to stream content directly from iTunes to their television sets. It was a clever idea in that prior to its introduction, the only way to get streaming video onto your TV set was to be tech-savvy enough to connect a dongle to your HDMI port with a cord long enough to reach the level spot you'd found to rest your laptop on. (And if you find yourself rolling your eyes at the notion that someone might not actually be able to do this, you'd be surprised.) It was also a notable step towards the widespread adoption of streaming video: the prior version of Apple TV relied on downloads.

The new Apple TV still offered a closed ecosystem, however. Only Apple-approved apps were allowed, and beyond iTunes and Netflix, there wasn't a whole lot available. Which was why the Roku box, originally conceived as a Netflix streaming device in 2008, began to get more attention.

Roku, whose square hockey puck size closely resembled the Apple TV's, revamped its line-up in September 2010 (around the same time as the relaunch of the Apple TV) to include WiFi enabled devices with HD quality streaming.

But Roku made two decisions that turned out to be very wise in the long-run. First, they introduced three models, the cheapest of which was priced at $50, half the price of the Apple TV. Second, they offered a wide range of channels: everything from Netflix, Hulu and Amazon to smaller streaming channels catering to niche audiences. Some of these niche channels were available via Roku's Channel Store, while others were only available as "private channels" accessible via an unpublicized website. These niche channels were to play an important role later on, but back in 2010 and 2011, it was the availability of sites like Vudu, Crackle, Epix, HBO GO, and others that helped make the relatively unknown Roku an attractive option.

While other manufacturers such as Western Digital and the now-defunct Boxee also made streaming boxes, the market quickly settled on Roku and Apple TV as the two main options.

Both devices helped popularize the growth of streaming video and made it easy for consumers to watch HD video on their HDTVs. Picture quality was equivalent to what viewers were getting from their pay TV providers, and the easy-to-navigate menus were a welcome change from the labyrinthine VOD menus the MVPDs featured. And at $50 to $99 a pop, it was easy enough to buy one for every TV in the house.

The growth of the streaming devices (whose joint numbers roughly paralleled those of Netflix) coincided with Netflix's shift from heavy movie content to heavy TV content. That made them more everyday devices than "movie night" devices and helped make them an integral part of the TV-watching experience in many homes.

I can't stress how important that last point is. Streaming started off as a niche market, and early Netflix was still a movie service, which meant the streaming device was something that got opened up on Saturday night. With the growth of TV content, streaming devices became an alternate set-top box and viewers were often struck by the difference between the elegant interfaces of the streaming boxes and the anything but elegant interfaces of their pay TV set-top boxes.

In July 2013, Apple TV and Roku were joined by the Google Chromecast device, a $35 "streaming stick" that plugged into the TV's HDMI port and streamed video from the Netflix, YouTube and other apps that viewers had on their smartphones, laptops and tablets. The device (and its low price point) were instant hits and Amazon quickly sold out of its first order of the thumb-sized devices. Chromecast offered a different take on the interface: rather than using the device as a set-top box alternative, Chromecast, unlike Apple TV and Roku, did not have a remote control, so viewers used the laptop, tablet or smartphone as the controller. Content was sent up to the cloud and then streamed to the Chromecast stick, which meant viewers could leave the app once they'd started the streaming process.

While it's a clever idea, it still has some kinks that need to be ironed out, especially for long-form content: if you need to pause the Chromecast once you've started watching a show, you need to go back to the app you launched it from to hit "pause." On a tablet with a dozen or so apps open, that's easier said than done. That's my reaction, anyway, others might argue that a generation that grows up without remote controls might not miss them, but I find myself missing one—or at least a dedicated top-level screen that serves as a remote, similar to the iPhone's one-swipe notification screen.

The final change to the streaming market came in April 2014, when Amazon launched their Fire streaming device. Priced at $99, the Fire is similar to both Roku and Apple TV in that it is a square hockey-puck-sized device that connects to the TV and is controlled by a separate remote. Its key differentiator is its ability to make use of voice commands. This was followed in October 2014 by the Fire Stick, a $39 device that was built to take on Chromecast.

Critical reaction was mixed: the larger Fire box was generally thought to be a few steps behind Roku, especially in terms of UX and amount of content. But the Fire Stick, the number-one selling item in Amazon's electronics store, was held to be superior, mostly due to the fact that it came with a remote.

Amazon frequently updates its projects, though, so we may see an improved version of both products in the near future.

GAMING DEVICES

Another group of players in the streaming ecosystem are gaming devices like Xbox and PlayStation. Xbox was the first entrant into the game when they introduced video apps to the new Xbox 360 in 2011. Xbox, Playstation and Nintendo's Wii are technically in excellent position to capture a large share of the streaming market as (a) they are already connected to the internet and (b) they have a large install base that is the envy of the MVPDs.

The idea with gaming devices is that they would become complete entertainment centers, with users seamlessly moving from playing Madden 2014 to watching the game on ESPNLive. Microsoft invested heavily in Xbox, introducing voice controls for video with the 2011 version along with an app called SmartGlass that provides second screen synchronicity with movies, shows and songs playing on XBox. (True Confession: I get no small amount of joy from watching movies on Xbox and saying "XBox pause. Xbox play" to control playback. It's so much easier than having to locate the remote. On the flip side, it seems like every time I turn it on, the Xbox needs to update Netflix or HBO Go, part of Microsoft's fabled user experience nightmare.)

The size of its subscriber base, coupled with Microsoft's active support, allowed Xbox to strike deals with a few dozen services, from mainstream customers like Netflix, Hulu, and Amazon to smaller studio-based plays and YouTube.

With the introduction of the Xbox One in 2013, many expected that the new device would allow users to set it up as a true set-top box, with the ability to run their pay TV system. That didn't happen, but Microsoft (and Sony and Nintendo) remain strong threats to the traditional set-top box, and it's quite possible that they will someday become the primary entertainment hub in most homes.

"Game console makers have long been amongst the most patient and aggressive investors in the promise of delivering TV services over the internet," notes consultant Brian Ring. "In fact, Microsoft & PlayStation have already racked up impressive consumer uptake despite plenty of blockers—a required subscription for the Xbox Live 'Gold' plan, awful authentication processes required for TV Everywhere, and a relative dearth of great content. I think console makers are poised to be big winners—especially since their powerful devices can provide a faster, more elegant lean-back interface for discovering content— something the TV makers will be hard pressed to replicate."

SMART TVs

The mass adoption of HDTV was both a blessing and a curse for TV manufacturers. The upside was that they were able to sell a lot more television sets as families migrated to the new technology. The downside was that the quality of the sets had reached a point where (particularly in the low and mid ends of the market) the picture quality more or less looked the same.

In order to create a point of difference (and, likely, to be able to get their hands on some portion of ad revenue) the major TV OEMs (original equipment manufacturers) began developing what they called "Smart TVs"—TVs with the ability to connect directly to the internet. These smart TVs came with pre-loaded apps, the most popular of which were ones that allowed viewers to connect directly to OTT services like Netflix, Hulu, or Amazon with just one click.

Sales of smart TV's have been very high, particularly in 2013 and 2014, but those numbers are very misleading. Lots of people own Smart TVs because that was what was on sale at Best Buy that week. But that doesn't mean they use them. As of May 2013, only 65% of Smart TV owners had even bothered to connect their sets to the internet, and once connected, there's no guarantee anyone is using it: the biggest slam on Smart TVs has been their clunky interface, leading many Smart TV owners to revert/resort to Rokus and Apple TVs.

The OEMs have not done themselves any favors either. In addition to clunky interfaces featuring way too many text-based apps like Facebook (many usability studies have shown that people don't like to read on big screens) they have not agreed on a standard interface, so that a Samsung Smart TV runs on a completely different system than one from LG.

This is a problem in that Americans own an average of three TV sets and replace them every seven years. So the odds of someone having three similarly aged TV sets from the same manufacturer are fairly slim.

Add in too the fact that the technology becomes outdated very quickly, far sooner than the seven-year life cycle consumers are expecting. While many of the newer sets are upgradeable, that's a fuzzy term: anyone with a laptop or smartphone knows that technology changes so rapidly that even "upgradeable" devices start to feel very outdated after three or four years.

Which is the Smart TV's greatest problem: consumers have figured out that it's much easier to buy a $50 Roku device they can replace every few years than to invest time and effort on a Smart TV that will soon be out of date. There's also the interoperability issue, not just between manufacturers but between models within a specific manufacturer. That's why I advise clients to put streaming devices in their roadmaps instead of Smart TVs. While an OEM may have a presence in tens of millions of homes, only a few hundred thousand of them will actually be able to make use of a new app. Compare that to Roku, Chromecast, and Apple TV, where you are immediately able to light up over twenty million homes. That's a huge difference.

There's also a bigger, philosophical issue around Smart TVs, one that has broader implications for the industry as a whole: Who controls the interface?

Will the interface of the future still come from the MVPDs who serve the broader role of content aggregator? Will they come from the TV set manufacturer? Or will they come from the streaming device itself? If I had to bet, I'd put my money on the MVPDs. In their roles as owners of the internet pipes, they have access to the greatest number of customers and as such, they can provide a standard that works on any device and with any TV. The caveat there (and it's a huge one) is that to date, the MVPDs have not shown much predilection for creating user-friendly interfaces. That leaves the door wide open for someone else to come in and innovate.

But there's a caveat to that caveat as well: TiVo tried this about fifteen years ago—their boxes had a far superior interface to the average set-top box, and they had another innovation: the DVR. For a while, they were the only game in town, but then the MVPDs started shipping set-top boxes with built-in DVRs, which they "rented" to consumers for a few dollars a month. The interfaces were all vastly inferior to TiVo, but the "rental" fee was much less than the monthly fee for TiVo and (more importantly) if they broke, the MVPD just sent you a new one. If your TiVo broke, it was your job to go and fix or replace it. Consumers overwhelmingly selected price and convenience over interface and there's no reason to think they won't go that route again. Yet another thing to keep an eye on over the next five to ten years.

There's one more possibility when thinking about who will eventually win the war for OTT and that's the MVPD set-top boxes themselves.

Netflix is already incorporated into all of Google Fiber's boxes and EPGs (electronic program guides—the grid with all the channels and shows on it) and is reputedly talking to other MVPDs as well. This makes way more sense than many observers realize. While the conventional wisdom of the tech blogosphere is that HBO made a brilliant move in splitting off (partially) from the TV Industrial Complex and launching itself as an independent brand like Netflix, the reverse moves actually makes more sense. Netflix no doubt looks at HBO and thinks "We wish we were you."

Who wouldn't want to be HBO? Every month Comcast, Charter, Dish, Uverse, et al. collect millions of dollars on its behalf—no call centers needed, no direct billing staff, no hassle of chasing down 28 million people every month. What's more, HBO is the beneficiary of frequent MVPD promotions—sign up now and get three free months of HBO. The assumption is that a goodly percentage of those viewers will continue their subscriptions, either because they like HBO or because they can't be bothered to figure out how to actually unsubscribe, a process the MVPDs have not made particularly easy. What's more, HBO benefits every time a viewer decides they want to watch *Homeland*. Which is on Showtime, but since the two networks are almost always bundled together, HBO benefits as well. If there are customer service issues with HBO, it's Comcast's fault, not HBO's. And if they raise their rates, well, I suspect Comcast will wind up getting the blame as well.

There's also the retention issue, which is something HBO does not seem to have fully considered: it's really hard to walk away from an MVPD bundle because the MVPDs make it hard to walk away. You get considerable savings from getting the titanium bundle, the one with the fastest internet speeds and all the premium cable stations bundled together. You can't pull out the HBO piece of the puzzle they've created without the whole stack crashing down and your monthly cost going up.

Contrast that with the ease with which a consumer can

subscribe and unsubscribe from a stand-alone service and HBO has reason to be worried. Mostly because HBO's content offering isn't strong enough to justify a year-long subscription.

Thanks to binge-viewing, users can knock off an entire season of *Game of Thrones* in about 3—4 weeks. And while HBO's movie offering is perfectly fine, they don't have the first-run movies that Amazon, iTunes, and Vudu do, and I don't know how many people are going to stick around to pay $10/month (or so) for the HBO OTT service just to watch their movies.

The binge-viewing part is what makes this seem so risky for HBO: back in the day, plenty of people would subscribe at the start of the *Sopranos* season and unsubscribe when it was over. But that was a six- or seven-month run. With binge-viewing, you can easily see viewers signing up for a month, two or three times a year, only to unsubscribe as soon as they'd watched the most recent series. A situation that could get worse should the industry start adopting Netflix's and Amazon's "all at once" theory of show release.

So it's not clear to me why HBO is so gung-ho on going it alone. Or why Netflix (whose vast selection of prior-season network TV series makes churn much less of an issue) wouldn't seek to try and become yet another premium channel in the MVPD line-up. The main hang-up for Netflix would be figuring out a way to get viewers into their interface from the MVPD's EPGs, but that's easily solved and the resulting solution would be user friendly as well.

One of the biggest complaints consumers have about their current set-up is that they constantly need to switch inputs as they move from live TV to OTT services. Collecting everything on the set-top box—or, conversely, on a gaming device— solves that problem. Yet one more thing to keep an eye on as it evolves.

SUMMARY

A range of options have cropped up to allow viewers to easily watch streaming (or "over the top") video. While phones and tablets are great back-up for personal viewing devices, the real magic happens on the 50+ inch HDTVs. There, streaming devices like Roku, Chromecast, Apple TV and the new

Amazon Fire TV seem poised to win out over Smart TVs, but an integrated set-top box or tablet-based app from the MVPD could be the final victor.

DISRUPTION POTENTIAL: 8.0

SECOND SCREEN AND SOCIAL TV

Quick question: When you're watching TV, do you talk during the entire show? When the commercials come on (provided you're not skipping through them) do you only think and talk about the show you've been watching?

I'm guessing the answer is no. So then why did so much of the initial activity in the social TV space assume the opposite?

Yes, a lot of people watch TV with a second screen device in hand. But there's no logical path that says they are using that device solely to interact with whatever is on the screen. Chances are high that if they've whipped out the iPhone, they are checking email, looking at a friend's Facebook photos, checking the score of the game they're not watching, or some other activity completely unrelated to the what's on TV.

ACTIVE VERSUS PASSIVE VIEWING

People often turn on the TV just to have some sort of background distraction. Call that "passive viewing." Reading email and half-watching *American Idol* aren't incompatible. Neither is going onto the Fox website and looking up the bio of a contestant who captures your attention. They're just two of the many things you might do during a passive viewing experience.

What about shows that aren't just background noise? Shows you look forward to and actually care about. Call that "active viewing." Logic dictates that if you are engrossed in a program, you are not going to wander off to look up the IMDB profile of the lead actor or open up TweetDeck to see if anyone else is tweeting about the District Attorney's pink shoes. That's something you are much more likely to do *after* the show, when you're done watching and have time to actually reflect on what you've just seen.

That's the thing about anything social: there are events where you want to spend the entire time talking exclusively about what is happening onscreen: football games, political debates, reality game show finales. But those are the exception, not the rule. During active viewing you're far more likely to give your undivided attention to what's happening on the screen, to the point of letting phone calls and texts go unanswered. During passive viewing, there's not a whole lot of incentive to spend any time talking about a program you're only casually watching.

Despite this, the ability to use a secondary device to either comment on or interact with something happening on the main screen, known as either "second screen" or "social TV" has been the subject of much buzz during the past few years, but the platform is still very much in its infancy.

The phenomenon was first called "social TV" as it involved fans tweeting during shows, and the early apps were just a way to collect those tweets and/or allow people to "check in" to TV shows to let their friends know what they were watching.

VCs in particular were very taken with the first round of social TV apps and funded many of them without ever stepping back to question the business plans (or lack thereof.)

Joining the "social TV" apps were so-called "second screen" apps that were not as time-dependent and allowed users to interact with shows or watch additional content on their own time. At a time when time-shifting is becoming more and more common, the idea of experiences that are not time-dependent has been well received.

One thing that emerged from the first round of Social TV was an understanding that different types of shows called for different types of interactions and that certain types of shows were more "social" than others.

Studies show that live sporting events and reality game shows were most likely to get fans interacting (either via Twitter or via polls and quizzes) during the show. This is not surprising if you consider the way people react in real life when these types of shows are on: they talk to each other and shout at the screen. Sporting events and reality game shows also feature lots of natural breaks (time outs, etc.), giving fans the opportunity to look away from the action on the main screen and type something on their second screen. What they're typing is (by and large) not all that time-intensive: "Go Nets!" or something similar is a lot quicker than trying to reduce a longer thought to 140 characters.

The other type of shows that get a lot of live interaction during the show are live event shows like the Super Bowl or the Oscars or even the presidential inauguration. These shows have the advantage of being watched live, in real time, by everyone, regardless of what time zone they are in. They also have lots of natural breaks and because they are spectacles, people feel compelled to talk about them. There are about a dozen or so shows that meet this definition, clustered around the beginning of the year (Super Bowl, Grammys, NBA All Star Game, Oscars, VMAs.)

Sitcoms and reality dramas (*Jersey Shore*, *Real Housewives*) fall into a middle category: there are some natural breaks that allow people to look away from the screen, but other than reacting to a particularly funny or outrageous line, there's not a whole lot to tweet about, and these sorts of shows don't automatically lend themselves to polls and quizzes.

The final category, dramas and crime shows, gets very limited social interaction as people are too wrapped up in the plot line to bother to look away from the screen. Again, this mirrors what happens in real life when people will "shush" anyone who interrupts them during a particularly high-intensity scene. There's also not much for people to talk about during commercial breaks— they're waiting for the action to start up again and don't want to risk missing something.

Where dramas and crime shows do get a lot of traction is after the show. That's when people want to discuss what just happened, to read recaps and reviews and continue their engagement with the show.

One of the more interesting things that turned up in some research I did while at Piksel was the fact that very few people (only 18%) said they exclusively watched their favorite programs live, with a much larger number (57%) saying they watched them exclusively either DVR'd or via On Demand. This seemed to indicate that people were cocooning with their favorite shows, watching them on their own time, during a period when they knew they'd have minimal interruptions.

That behavior seemed to indicate that the market for second screen content would be around experiences that happened after (or before) the show and appealed to hard core fans of the show rather than casual viewers.

This has always been the debate around second screen and social TV: is the ultimate business value to content owners the ability to attract new fans and drive tune-in or is it to create a stronger bond with the show's hardcore fans who will then go on to become evangelists for the show?

This does not have to be an either/or proposition. The USA Network had great success driving tune-in for its hit show *Psych* by organizing fans and getting them to post on social media prior to special episodes

"We had several goals for the campaign," relates Jesse Redniss, founder of media consultancy BRaVe Ventures, who was Senior Vice President of Digital at USA Networks at the time. "We wanted to drive tune-in by leveraging the existing fan base and have their social activity have a halo effect to also drive new audience tune-in too. The key was to use a diversified audience engagement strategy to go where the fans were on social. It wasn't just about Twitter. We used several platforms including Facebook, Shazam, Instagram and Beamly. We constantly measured and recalibrated too. The combination of platforms proved to be incredibly effective since the show audience across social media is still very fragmented and you want to reach fans where they are most comfortable and actively participating with a community."

Similarly, event shows like the Grammys and the Oscars have seen lift from the amount of social media buzz happening around the event.

THE RISE OF SECOND SCREEN 2.0

2013 and 2014 were not good years for the first round of players in the second screen industry. Many went out of business as consumers showed little interest in checking in to shows or getting recommendations from apps that couldn't tell them what channel the show was on. Those that did survive kept merging until almost none were left.

What emerged, though, was the second wave of second screen, call it Second Screen 2.0. Rather than being all about apps, 2.0 is all about the data that's collected from second screen experiences that take place on Facebook, Twitter,Tumblr, Instagram, Snapchat, Pinterest, and a host of network OTT apps. The data is valuable because it's gleaned from individual users, not households. And because so much of it is gleaned from social platforms, it's easy to learn what else the viewer likes, what their friends like, and how that plays out across their social graph.

TV networks are using that data in four distinct ways:

- To gain and sustain audience
- To make programming decisions
- To give advertisers a better understanding of their audience
- To aid in discovery

TWITTER BOUNCES BACK

Twitter has always been the obvious platform for social TV. It's public, it's short and it's easy to organize tweets around a topic using hashtags.

But Twitter's current user base is fairly limited and doesn't show much sign of growing: somewhere between 20% and 25% of Americans use it on a regular basis. That's 75% to 80% that don't see any of the activity on Twitter. What's more, Twitter's user base is concentrated in a few niche demographics, which is why the list of the most tweeted-about shows rarely intersects with the list of the highest rated shows.

And while Twitter activity is heavy around so called "tent pole" or event shows, for everything else it's fairly banal, consisting mostly of "Yo. Watching American Dad. Yo." "How was that a foul?" "Penny is hawt" and similarly deep comments.

That's why I've often said that Twitter did an excellent job of convincing people outside the TV industry that it played a major role within the industry. (Especially right before it's IPO.) In fact, a recent study done by Piksel and Streaming Media showed that only 13% of respondents were "active Twitter users" while watching TV.

But that's about to change.

In what promises to be a major breakthrough for the platform, Twitter is going to begin allowing tweets to runs as native advertising on third party sites. And here's why that's huge: people may not necessarily like Twitter. (In fact, many of them hate it.) But they care what's being said on Twitter. And that's the genius of surfacing those "tweet ads" on third party sites: they bring what's being said on Twitter to the 75% of the population that doesn't use it.

Consciously or subconsciously, Twitter is finally acknowledging what it is: a broadcasting platform rather than a social network. The tweet opens up a world of possibility for the television industry to use Twitter as a tune-in and loyalty driver.

Not that they haven't tried before. The television industry gave Twitter billions of dollars worth of free promotion by running tweets on screen for everything from news shows to sitcoms.

So what's different this time?

Interactivity. Twitter is an interactive medium. And on television that interactivity got lost. You couldn't click on links, see photos, watch videos. All you were left with was 140 characters of random degrees of cleverness.

By putting the tweet ads on third-party sites, Twitter has even taken steps to ensure that interactivity matters. Take native video: rather than rely on Vine or YouTube, Twitter now lets users pack 30 seconds' worth of video into every tweet. That's an entire TV commercial showing up as a native ad. With 140 characters of explanation and a link you can click on.

This gives networks the ability to push tweets from the show itself, the showrunner, a character, a popular actor, or even other fans onto apps and sites where the audience is most likely to see them.

Twitter recently added a native video feature too, which allows networks to attach a 30 second clip to their tweets to further tease audiences. That's perfect for attracting mobile users, as "tweet ads" have the ability to run on both desktop and mobile, even inside apps.

Thanks to another innovation—a deal with Google that allows tweets to show up in search results, the tweet ads will gain a second life, attracting potential viewers who are looking for information about a show and providing them with video clips, photos, and previews, all of which should help drive the long tail.

The biggest boon, though, will come from the data that's gathered from the tweet ads. Networks will be able to see which tweets got the most clickthough, the most video views, the most retweets, the most shares, and then learn who was engaging, what sites, during what times and around what content. They'll also be able to see which messaging seemed to affect ratings and then adjust for the following week.

That's a powerful toolset, one that's never been available to the television industry before.

Tweet ads can also open up new revenue streams: networks can now sell co-branded tweets that run in tandem with commercials, giving brands the ability to enjoy the halo effect of the show in a format that's not interruptive. And since tweet ads will be clickable, there's an interactive element that should also please advertisers. Here again, the data that's collected will be of great value both to the network, as it shapes its ad pitch, and to advertisers as they shape their marketing message.

Tweet ads can even be used to cross-promote shows: networks can have their most popular franchises tweet about new shows, providing video clips to entice viewers and again, using the data collected to better understand their audience.

Two new Twitter tools—Curator, an app for pushing out curated tweet lists and Niche, a social media star talent agency—give Twitter even more publishing chops: they can provide a complete 360 experience, including the talent to create and bring messages to life. That's something television networks can't do, and it gives Twitter a very powerful advantage in the coming war for eyeballs.

FACEBOOK AND VIDEO

Facebook has the mass audience that Twitter lacks, but much of the activity on Facebook is private. While the platform has experimented with surfacing anonymized data to the various networks and MVPDs, the fact remains that people rarely post about what show they are currently watching. Facebook tends to be an after-the-fact tool and it's rare that interactions happen in real time; it's far more likely that someone posts a comment about the latest episode of a favorite TV series and over the course of a day or two their friends who also watch the series debate and discuss that comment. It's a system that's well suited to asynchronous, time-shifted viewing as people can join in after they've finished watching (versus Twitter which relies almost exclusively on real-time interactions). But the very features that make Facebook appealing to its users (private conversations among friends) are also the features that make it less useful as a discovery tool: people care what certain members of their group of friends are talking about, not necessarily what an agglomeration of groups of friends are discussing.

There's also the problem with what people "Like" on Facebook. In fact, the more I use Facebook Graph Search, the more evident it becomes that Facebook made a major mistake with their most ubiquitous feature.

Follow this train: Facebook's value, their kryptonite, is their data. They have a billion users, and they know the habits and preferences of all billion of them because they can easily track that information by examining what they've Liked.

Or can they?

On the pre-Like Facebook, users were fans of pages. That information—which brands, bands, books, movies, sports teams, etc. a user was a fan of—was prominently displayed on the user's profile page. Which meant users spent a lot of time curating those selections, pruning and adding so that the list was an accurate reflection of who they were. Or at least who they wanted people to think they were.

As a result, it was tough (or tough-ish) to get users to become fans of pages they didn't think would give them social currency or look good on their wall. Hence, the Like—an easy way to give a brand a thumbs-up (and permission to coat your wall with brand messages).

But while the Like button has become ubiquitous and a seeming smash hit for Facebook, it does not appear to be used in any consistent manner. That was its selling point: a lower key way for users to indicate approval for a brand, but it's also its Achilles' heel: if users aren't displaying any sort of consistency in the way they use the like button, then the resulting data is fairly inaccurate and not all that useful. (Bye-bye monetization.)

This is evident in the spate of Tumblr blogs flagging the random overlaps Facebook Graph Search pulls up (married men who like prostitutes, Christians who like porn) and in less quirky uses, like the study BTIG did on the accuracy of using Graph Search as a movie recommendation engine. What they found should be somewhat troubling for Facebook: the movies users Liked overwhelmingly dated back to the list they compiled when they first signed up for the service or to when they last used the Fan format.

There are multiple reasons users are either promiscuous or inconsistent with their Likes, but they all circle around two competing forces: If The Brands We Like are how we present ourselves to the world, it takes a lot for a new brand to crack that list, and if Likes are easy to give and easily buried in the News Feed, there's no reason not to give them out at random.

Now by brands, I mean any sort of product: movies, books, songs, actors, vacation spots, along with the more typical products and services we call brands. To the consumer, they're all a part of who they are, and attaching their name to anything other than the tried and true, when that preference is in a prominent location, is a leap.

The constant rejiggering of the Facebook interface—particularly the introduction of the Timeline, where the "About" section, with the brands and media the user likes, is now one level down—has lessened the amount of attention people give to their Likes. That in turn, works on the validity of Likes from another direction: those who don't see their Likes as a reflection of who they are, will be likely to become more promiscuous with them, and at the same time more random, on the assumption that the action has both an immediate value (unlocking a coupon offer) and limited aftereffects.

While it's possible to imagine a scenario where Facebook encourages users to carefully parse out Likes to new products so that their opinions can help guide their friends, it seems unlikely:

first and foremost there is the black-and-white nature of the Like: it's an endorsement, pure and simple, in the way that three stars out of five is not.

Can Facebook fix this? Probably. They'll need to rethink both the Like and frictionless sharing and the value users place on having their brand and media preferences prominently featured on their profiles. If they can solve for that in a way that encourages more, rather than less interaction, and more curation of the brands (media and otherwise) a user Likes, they have a good chance to make their data more accurate and thus, more valuable.

The stakes are high though, and it's a big if.

Which is not to count Facebook out of the second screen race, though. Far from it. Facebook's value is going to be as a tune-in vehicle, perhaps the most effective one the networks will have.

It all hinges on Facebook's new video ad network: by parsing data about what shows viewers have already "Liked" on Facebook with other online behaviors (sites visited, purchases made, other "Likes," etc.) and mixing in data from their Friend lists on both Instagram and Facebook, Facebook can now offer networks a targeted TV promotions platform.

Imagine ABC being able to push out a 30-second promo for *Modern Family* to millions of targeted viewers on Facebook and Instagram an hour before the program is due to air. That would be a powerful experience considering that video uploaded natively to Facebook autoplays in users' News Feeds which creates a very noticeable ad unit. Especially if the video is configured in a way that catches viewers attention with the sound off. (Facebook's autoplay feature wisely keeps the sound off until the user clicks on it.) Facebook also announced plans to allow viewers to embed Facebook videos on third-party sites (which would then allow users to comment via their Facebook log-ins). That will give Facebook videos even greater reach and allow networks and shows to use Facebook as their home page for video content.

Facebook video is just the start, too. Nielsen will soon be including Facebook video in its Online Ratings, and companies like Synacor are enabling Facebook authentication for pay-TV providers so viewers can tie Facebook accounts to their provider's TV Everywhere apps. That means that once a user sees an ad on Facebook, they will be able to click through to watch the series on their tablet, phone, PC, or even stream it to their TV using a device like Chromecast or Roku.

All of this combines to give Facebook the ability to not just be the primary driver of live tune-in, but the primary viewing platform as well. From Nielsen's Online Campaign Ratings, to the networks ability to cull data surrounding viewing habits and integration capabilities, this is a comprehensive approach that should make Facebook a real force in the TV industry.

While Facebook has stumbled in the past when dealing with user privacy concerns, the platform has (hopefully) learned from prior missteps and will be able to keep user fears at bay. Which is why the MVPDs should be keeping a very close eye on how quickly Facebook and the various broadcast and cable networks realize that an alliance is in their best interests.

TUMBLR CATCHES UP

Tumblr is the real outlier here. A recent study revealed that there was more activity on Tumblr than on any other social platform if you look at activity over an 11 day window (five days before and five days after the initial broadcast date.

That makes perfect sense in that Tumblr blogs are often maintained by hardcore fans who create animated gifs, collages and other visuals out of key scenes from the show that are then shared with other hardcore fans, people who speak the same language and know all of the fan base's memes. It's a very different dynamic than what you'll find on Twitter or Facebook where the people commenting tend to be less committed to the show itself and more committed to broadcasting on social media.

The hardcore fans on Tumblr form a key audience however, as they are the ones who will continue to be involved with the show for years to come, possibly even funding reunion movies and the like as we'll see in the chapter on Fan Communities.

SNAPCHAT: THE YOUNG MILLENNIAL PLATFORM

Long dismissed as a place for teenage sexting, the entire industry seems to have woken up to the fact that Snapchat is the most popular platform for teenagers, supplanting Facebook and

Instagram.

Networks have started to use it for promotions too: MTV announced the VMA nominees via a series of snaps earlier this year and *Pretty Little Liars* has also used Snapchat to give fans access to plot twists.

Snapchat is unique in terms of engagement because users have to actively click on anything that's pushed out to them—things don't just show up in their feeds. That's both a curse and a blessing, but it means that anyone who is actually interacting with the message is doing so on purpose because they want to see it. That's going to keep showrunners on their toes in terms of what they're putting out there: it's got to be good enough for fans to keep wanting to watch it. Which means for those who get it right, Snapchat is going to be a powerful audience-retention vehicle.

THE FOUR S'S

While much of the talk around second screen focuses on the "social" content that users will create, that's just the tip of the iceberg: most users don't want to create content of any sort and are more than happy to let someone else do that for them. "Someone else," in this instance being the people who create the actual shows, and/or the networks and the advertisers who pay to be on those networks.

In talking to all of the aforementioned stakeholders, I've come to the conclusion that second screen content can be broken out into four main buckets. Their weight in the second screen experience will vary from show to show, depending on factors like audience makeup and content type. The mix may even vary depending on when the viewer experiences it: before, during, or after the program.

These four content buckets, which we've been calling the "4 S's" are Social, Stories, Stats, and Shopping.

Social is social media, which will play an increasingly shrinking role in the equation. While Twitter currently has a large install base compared to any dedicated second screen experience, it is nowhere near as ubiquitous as many advocates would have us believe: the majority of Americans are not on Twitter and are unlikely to ever join. Even among Twitter users, influence varies wildly depending on content: for every Oscar ceremony, there are 10 documentaries on the Military Channel no one is tweeting about. The waning popularity of live television makes any "of the moment" form of social media less relevant. Which is perhaps why a recent study showed that "only 1.5% of respondents report being drawn to TV-viewing occasions because of social media." Social will continue to be important for sports and other event programming that people like to watch live, but I see its current prominence rapidly diminishing, particularly for scripted programming.

Stories will become the most prominent second screen content for scripted programming. Stories, which will be created by the same people who create the show itself (with occasional help from avid fans), can be anything from "scenes from next week" to behind the scenes footage to interviews with the stars or producers to additional background on the characters. This content will generally be intended to be viewed either before or after the show—not during it. It's ideal for hardcore fans and for viewers who are bingeing on a show and want to catch up on the entire experience. The advantage for networks and advertisers is that this is the sort of content fans will return to long after the program airs live, thus prolonging exposure to the series itself and providing additional opportunities for both advertising and promotion of other network shows. It's also a potential gathering point for super fans, something we'll explore in more detail in a subsequent chapter.

Stats are statistics, polls, voting, and all other things number based. These will be particularly important for sports and reality game shows, where viewer interaction is already part of the experience. Being able to touch the screen to manipulate stats and poll results and the like should prove to be a very engaging experience and this is one area where users will be able to take full advantage of their devices. As a result, stats should prove more popular during programming that is watched live than during scripted programming.

Shopping is t-commerce, which will generally happen after the viewer is done watching the show. Certain types of how-to shows (cooking and home improvement) may prove to be the exceptions, but given that many of those shows are, for all intents and purposes, 30-minute infomercials as it is, providing a vehicle for in-show t-commerce makes perfect sense. For scripted programming, however, it's something that is likely to occur once the program is over and the viewer has time to focus on shopping, rather than cramming it in during a quick commercial break, or, as the infamous "Jennifer Aniston's Sweater" example has it, during the actual program itself. If done correctly, t-commerce can be an integral part of a very lucrative second screen ad ecosystem.

Showrunners will need to figure out what combination of the " Four S's" best suits the needs of their audience, and then tweak that content-- on a daily basis, if necessary. The goal of the content will be multi-fold and will vary from show to show, but the key objectives will be to drive tune-in, increase loyalty among hard core fans, promote future episodes, and to serve as an advertising platform, thus opening up a second revenue stream. (In addition, as live TV viewing decreases, networks will need to seek out alternate ways to promote their new shows. Second screen experiences for their existing shows should prove to be an effective medium.)

IT'S ALL ABOUT THE SHOWRUNNER

For all the debate around who should be in charge of second screen and social TV efforts, one thing is becoming very clear: the key to success rests with the showrunners.

That's because when the showunner is involved, along with the actors and the writing staff, it seems like the second screen experience is an actual part of the show, not some sort of bolted-on afterthought. In fact, a recent study done by Twitter, Fox and the Advertising Research Foundation revealed that 40 percent of viewers prefer to see tweets from cast members versus 18 percent who wanted to see tweets from the official show handle.

This stands to reason on many levels: the type of viewer who is fan enough to want to tweet or post about a show is the type of viewer who's likely formed some sort of connection with the actors and wants to read their tweets. It gives the sense of having a conversation with the actor, and if the actor responds to or favorites a tweet, even better.

To be successful at second screen, the production company needs to think through everything from how to translate the for a gaming platform to what sort of content to feature for behind-the-scenes, backstory or alternative storylines to how to film all of it, when and why. Then, once they've figured that all out, they need to figure out whose job it is to make sure everything gets done.

It's a lot more complicated than just pulling together a couple of stills for the website and letting an intern wander around with a camera shooting "behind the scenes" footage.

But it's worth it because when it's done right, it feels authentic and even more important, it feels organic—like everything is a part of the same show.

It's worth it because the people who watch the show months, maybe even years, after it first airs are going to want a way to engage with the show, to talk about it, learn about it, to essentially recreate the water cooler chatter they long missed out on. And the strength of that second screen engagement is going to play a big role in propelling them from watching just one episode to watching the entire series

It's worth it, too, because second screen creates an additional advertising platform and thus an additional revenue stream, which more than makes up for the time and effort spent on creating that second screen experience.

But it's got to start with the showrunners. Third-party apps and network apps have their place, but they're only as good (and desirable) as the content that's on them. If the experiences around the shows are things fans want to engage with, then they'll take off. But if the experiences are just IMDB, Rotten Tomatoes and a Twitter feed, that tells fans "we don't really care about you" and those fans will take their loyalty to a show whose second screen experience says otherwise.

IT'S ALL ABOUT THE DATA

The next wave of second screen, second screen 2.0, is all about the data. Data is going to be the currency that fuels the entertainment industry in the years ahead, and second screen will be the way that data is collected.

People routinely give up their personal information to apps and games online when they choose the "log in with Facebook" option. So why would entertainment properties be any different? And as second screen interactions increasingly take place through social platforms, viewers will be providing content owners with a wide range of valuable data.

Second screen data is valuable to content owners in three different ways:

1. Gaining and Maintaining Audience: second screen data allows showrunners to see who their audience is so they can figure out ways to attract new viewers and keep current ones. It can be as simple as using Facebook data to determine viewers who are most likely to watch a show because (a) many of their friends do and (b) they've liked similar shows and then making sure video promotions appear in their feeds.

Sustaining audiences is even easier: it's about using data on what segments generated the most buzz and making sure that their second screen content reflects their viewers' preferences.

2. Making Programming Decisions. Second screen data is a great way to see what resonates with viewers and which viewers it resonates with. So if a show wants to appeal more to women or to a younger demo, the showrunners can glean information about what's working with those segments and use that to inform future episodes.

There's a danger, of course, with allowing data to have too much influence over scripts: viewers notoriously stick to the tried and true and new ideas take a while to gain traction. Deciding when and where to use data is a balancing act each showrunner must perform for themselves.

3. Identifying Advertising Opportunities. Networks can use second screen data to get a much clearer view of who their audiences are and what other brands they're interested in. They can then use that data to create more effective ad buy opportunities, steering advertisers to the particular audience segments they want. That same data can be used to strike other types of deals too, such as product placement and joint promotions. Finally, the networks themselves can use the data to help cross-promote their own shows to audiences who are likely to want to see them.

4. Improving Recommendations and Discovery. By knowing which shows a particular viewer has interacted with (saved to a

watch list, shared to social media, participated in a contest) and cross-referencing that with their friends activity and the demographic and psychographic profiles of people who like certain shows, we will be able to make much better recommendations as to what types of shows and movies a viewer might like, based not just on title, but also on location and time of day.

What makes second screen data so valuable is that viewers are not responding to pre-canned questions, which often leads to questionable results. They are, rather, offering up their own thoughts and feelings, which makes the data far more authentic.

The other unique aspect of second screen data is that it's collected from individual users, not from households. That gives anyone analyzing it a much clearer view of who is doing what, when, where, how, and (possibly) why. That's data the TV industry never had before and, given the rapidly changing landscape, it will prove to be invaluable in the years ahead.

"If there is anything that is going to drive second screen forward, it is data," says Guy Finley, Executive Director of the second Screen Society, a trade organization I am currently Chairman of. "There is so much value in analyzing second screen transactions and understanding what people are doing and why. It lets everyone make smarter decisions."

SUMMARY:

Second Screen 1.0 was all about apps, but viewers didn't seem to find them particularly compelling. Second Screen 2.0 is all about existing social platforms and the data that can be collected from them. That data can be used to build and maintain audiences, make smarter programming decisions, and create more targeted advertising opportunities. Just as important, it provides the television industry with insights it never had before.

DISRUPTION POTENTIAL: 9.5

FANS AND FAN COMMUNITIES

A few years back, a friend of mine wrote a video for Funny Or Die called "Café Attitude." I thought the actor who played the waiter in the clip really nailed the scene and wondered what else he'd been in.

So I googled "Gale Harold" and promptly fell down the proverbial rabbit hole.

For while I was aware that there were fan communities, some of whom were quite passionate, I was not in any way prepared for the volume.

Harold, a multi-talented actor, who has since become a close friend, has had leading roles in a number of series ranging from *Desperate Housewives* to *Deadwood* to *The Secret Circle*. But it was his role in the Showtime series *Queer As Folk*, which ran from 2000 to 2005, that was still generating an extraordinary amount of activity. There were still, all these years later, vibrant fan communities around the show, fueling everything from message boards to Tumblr blogs to fan fiction forums to Twitter feeds devoted exclusively to photos of Harold. Tens of thousands of fans, all deeply involved with a show that had been off the air for almost a full decade.

It's not just *Queer As Folk*: there are close to a hundred U.S. TV shows that have passionate online fan bases. Take *Veronica Mars*, for instance. The show, which follows the adventures of a teenage detective, was moderately popular when it first ran on UPN (later the CW) from 2004 to 2007. But fans kept the spirit alive on the internet and in 2013, series creator Rob Thomas launched a Kickstarter campaign to fund a Veronica Mars movie. They raised the requested $2 million dollars in just 10 hours—winding up with $5,702,153 from 91,585 donors. As a result the Veronica Mars movie—with almost all the original cast—was in theaters in March of 2014.

"It was a long road," relates Ivan Askwith, who served as Associate Producer on the film and oversaw the Kickstarter campaign and managed the ongoing relationship between the fans, cast, and creative team. "Fans never stopped asking Rob and Kristen for a movie, but it wasn't that simple. They had to get Warner Brothers [who held the rights to the show] to agree, and then had to actually go out and raise the money."

For Askwith, who'd studied fan communities under noted professor Henry Jenkins at MIT, working on the Veronica Mars movie was a dream come true, as it allowed him to put into practice many of the theories he'd developed as a graduate student.

Askwith believes that there is money to be made in catering to fan communities and that niche content presents an opportunity for exploring alternate business models.

He outlined the history of fans efforts to save their favorite entertainment properties, a behavior that dates back to pre-internet days. One of the first notable efforts took place in 1968, when *Star Trek* fans protested the possible cancellation of the series after its second season. That, and the fact that the series was near the magic number of 100 episodes needed for syndication, are believed to be the main reasons that *Trek* lived to see a third and final season.

A more recent example of a fan base coming to the rescue of a show was the CBS television series *Jericho*. In 2007, when CBS announced the show was being cancelled after the first season, members of several online fan communities started a campaign to revive the series. Their efforts included sending over 20 tons of nuts to CBS headquarters (a reference to a key line in the show). Their plan worked, and the show was renewed for a second season, and while it did not make it to the third, it was a sign of how powerful the voice of fans could be—and this was before the massive growth of social media.

Fans raised their voices again in 2009, when NBC seemed close to canceling the action-comedy/spy-drama *Chuck*. Fans realized they needed to prove the link between their passion and revenue, so they targeted Subway, which had been a major sponsor of the show, congregating en masse at Subway stores and filling out comment cards stating that if Subway supported *Chuck*, they would support Subway.

As a result, Subway agreed to sponsor the series, and NBC renewed it. Subsequent seasons of *Chuck* featured frequent and conspicuous references to Subway and their sandwiches, which Askwith explained became sort of an in-joke with the fan community. "Usually, product placement is a nuisance. But since the show's most devoted fans knew that Subway had saved their show, these placements were interpreted as a fun inside joke—and a reminder of the show's debt to the brand."

Veronica Mars represented the first real test to see if fan communities could actually put up the (not inconsiderable) production costs involved in making a movie or television show. This is a part of the story that many in the tech community forget. As I often find myself saying, the reason the television industry is not like the music business is because to make a great song you need someone with an instrument and a good voice. To make a great TV show, you need at least a million dollars.

Once the Kickstarter campaign was launched, Askwith worked closely with Thomas and the production company to explain their value proposition while responding directly to audience questions and concerns. "It was natural for people to think that once we'd hit our original goal, that any extra money was pure profit going into the studio's pocket. We needed to explain that the more money we raised, the better the overall production would be."

Keeping fans involved and feeling like they were part of the process was one of Askwith's goals, and he received full support from both the cast and the production company. Ninety-three high-level backers were given the opportunity to work as extras on the film, and their experiences were broadcast back to the community. Actors participated in an online viewing marathon as fans watched episodes of the TV show, answering questions and sharing memories. Through Askwith, the cast and writers also provided regular updates from the set, as well as behind-the-scenes photos from each day of production.

For Askwith, the ultimate moment came when fans were participating in MTV's "Movie Brawl" contest (making sure Veronica Mars stayed ahead of the competition) and kept referring to it as "our movie" not "the movie."

"In entertainment marketing, you always talk about wanting evangelists and super fans, but this took that to a totally different level," he notes. "Our backers felt *responsible* for the success of the movie."

The confluence of social media, crowdfunding, and fan communities has given actors, writers, and showrunners the ability to establish direct relationships with their audiences in a way that was not previously possible.

The more active an artist is on social media, the more likely it is that they can help bring an audience to their next project. "The size of your Twitter following is definitely something producers take note of," says Scott Lowell (another close friend) who starred along with Harold in *Queer As Folk,* and is currently starring along with Bradley Cooper in the Broadway and West End revivals of *The Elephant Man.* "Any time I'm in a new production, whether it's a movie or a play, I can spread the word to almost ten thousand people, who can then tell their friends about it too. That's a big plus."

In large part due to his strong social media presence, Lowell has become the de facto liaison between the *Queer As Folk* cast and the fan community, both online and at "cons," conventions where fans travel from far and wide to meet the actors. *Queer As Folk's* fan base surprisingly is almost exclusively female. "That was something that was happening while the show was on the air," Lowell explains. "The producers and Showtime wanted to broaden the show's appeal, and the plot lines seemed to resonate with a female audience." Lowell understands why some actors would hesitate to become so tied to a single role but thinks a lot of that has to do with how you spin it. "Look, if a show was part of your life for five or six years, that's a pretty big chunk of time. And if you embrace your fans from that period and enlist them to help make your new projects successful, it seems like a win-win to me."

Thanks to crowdfunding sites like Kickstarter and IndieGoGo, actors now have the ability to fund their own projects. Chris Lowell (no relation to Scott), one of the leads in Veronica Mars, was able to raise over $200,000 from fans, way beyond his initial $65,000 goal, to help finish his indie film project *Beside Still Waters.*

There is a flip side to this new media paradigm however. "There are many new platforms where you can connect to and interact with your audience, so many new places where people can find both you and your work," notes Gale Harold. "It can be both liberating and disruptive because maintaining an online presence, managing the new platforms, and actively taking part in them can be quite time-consuming. So suddenly time you once spent on your craft, on your art, is now given over to managing these accounts, and at times, that can be extremely counterproductive."

THE LONG TAIL

What's potentially disruptive about the fan communities is the opportunity to monetize shows long after they've gone off air and to create a "long tail" source of revenue for everyone involved in the show, from actors to writers to producers.

David B. Williams, currently chief technology and content strategist for Endemol Beyond, was involved in one of the first fan cultivation efforts around the early 2000s Showtime hit *The L Word* and is well versed in the world of fan communities. "There's so much opportunity," Williams notes, "so long as the efforts remain authentic. Fans are very much attuned to any sign of inauthenticity, of feeling like they're being manipulated. Engaging them is like playing with fire. While they can provide essential heat, light, and drive, they can also blow up in your face."

One possibility Williams mentions is that cult hits that don't quite have the ratings to sustain a network TV presence can live on as web series, perhaps with shorter episodes. He also sees the reverse as possible: web series with strong fan bases getting picked up by cable networks.

"A hardcore audience is a powerful thing," Williams notes. "They'll stick with a show and the characters, and they're much less concerned with where it winds up than with the fact that it's still alive and kicking."

Today, showrunners have to start thinking about what they could do with fan communities from the very beginning, how to bring them along between seasons, and most important, how to keep them engaged once the show is no longer on the air. The latter piece assumes greater importance as services like Netflix continue to grow, giving a new generation of fans the opportunity to discover popular series like *Lost* and *The Sopranos*.

Given that most shows shot during the 2000s were shot in HD, they don't have that dated look that plagues shows from earlier decades. And so as a new generation discovers them, they'll join the existing fan base and create opportunities to both extend the story and make money off of it. Throw in international fans who may come to the series a few years after Americans, and there's even more volume.

This brand extension can benefit everyone from a successful series as fans can be called upon to help support future projects from the show's actors, writers, producers, and directors.

And then there's the content the fans create themselves.

FAN FICTION

No chapter on fan communities would be complete without a look into the phenomenon of fan fiction which is a much, much larger phenomenon than most non-participants realize. It's a growing and multi-faceted world, with it's own lingo, rules, and superstars. There are tens of thousands of people writing fan fiction and hundreds if not thousands of websites devoted to it. There are even success stories: the best-selling series *Fifty Shades of Grey* started out as a *Twilight* fan fiction and was reworked so that the characters were independent creations, not characters from the series. Amazon even has an entire section— Kindle Worlds— devoted to fan fiction stories.

Since *Queer As Folk* was the rabbit hole I first stumbled down, that's the fan fic world I first explored. Where I learned terms like "slash fic" which means that the story involves a homosexual relationship between two characters who may or may not have been involved in canon (the actual show that aired) and who may or may not even have been interested in members of that sex, (homosexual relationships between characters who were portrayed as heterosexual in canon is a major theme of slash fiction, which is mostly written by heterosexual women. Some of the original slash fic involved Kirk and Spock from *Star Trek*.)

There's also "mpreg," which stands for "male pregnancy" and involves a male character getting impregnated by another male character via a homosexual encounter and carrying the baby to term (e.g., Kirk knocks up Spock. And if you think I'm making that one up, just google "mpreg").

The "fan girls" and "fan boys" (many more of the former than the latter) who write and comment on these fanfics are also known as "shippers" (short for "worshippers") of specific characters/couples on the show. "AU" stands for "alternate universe" which means the author has introduced new characters or plot lines that deviate from canon. AUs may put the characters in different eras and locations, even play with their ages. The key is that the characters continue to have the personalities they have in canon. (Unless, of course, the author offers a reason why the character is acting differently—e.g., Spock gets hit on the head by a meteor and becomes illogical.)

But here's what really amazed me about the fan fics I read: many of them were pretty good. A few, very good. Not as in giving Alice Walker a run for her money good, but they were well-written and well-paced, with believable dialogue and plot lines—certainly on par with many of the romance and detective stories you see crowding the best seller lists. What's more, many of the readers left thoughtful and insightful criticism for the authors, no worse than feedback I'd gotten in upper-level creative writing workshops in college.

The genre has even evolved to the point where there are satires of typical fan fiction tropes and meta-stories where the characters are actually commenting on their fan-fictional selves. (For a brilliant scholarly view of the world of fan fiction, check out Henry Jenkins' work *Textual Poachers: Television Fans and Participatory Culture*.)

So what's the takeaway here?

Fandom is a huge untapped market. Hardcore fans aren't just hitting "Like" on Facebook or tweeting out that they're watching this week's episode. They're creating things: stories, gifs, memes, Tumblr blogs. Which means that every show with a hardcore fan base has a built-in audience of evangelists available to extend the story for years after the show goes off the air. They just need to be treated with respect: these fans are creating their work for themselves and for other fans. Not for the world at large. Which makes them different than the fans on Twitter. But different in a good way: they're far more loyal and committed. Engaging them starts with the show's creators, writers, and actors acknowledging their commitment and their passion and the fact that they've often created something more substantial than a 140-character check in and goes from there.

"The ability to identify and harness fan communities with digital efficiency has forever changed the media landscape," Williams adds. "For a producer, the big trick with fan communities is figuring out how to motivate that 1% of the audience to create content that will be compelling to the remaining 99%. Most fan creations come and go like a tree falling in the forest with no one to hear."

Fandom, and the degree to which (if handled correctly) fans are financially invested in the show's success, points to the viability of models other than the traditional advertising-based models, which rely on mass audiences. Niche content can be financially viable when there is a strong fan base that is willing to pay for it. And it's time that the industry realized that there are many shows that can generate this type of enthusiasm. And that these fans are happy to contribute. Or as the meme inspired by the *Futurama* character Fry succinctly puts it, "Shut up and take my money!"

That means it may be possible for shows with passionate fan bases to live on online, rather than on linear television. For while they may not draw the audiences that entice national advertisers, they do have the ability to draw in enough fans who'll pay to finance production costs and that in turn may be enough to attract sponsors who'll enjoy those fans' increased loyalty.

That also frees up the shows creatively. One of the most interesting things Askwith told me was that he was unconcerned that the movie had received mixed reviews from critics. "It was a hit with the fans, with the people who helped finance the movie," he said. "That's who we made it for and that's whose opinion we cared about."

SUMMARY:

Passionate fan communities exist for hundreds of shows, including many that are no longer on the air. These communities are very committed, very active, and they're willing to spend money to continue their involvement with the show. These fan communities can also be mobilized to help promote new seasons or upcoming episodes, but they need to be handled gingerly. Social media has given actors the ability to mobilize their fan bases to support their new projects, either via Twitter and other social platforms or via crowdfunding sites like Kickstarter.

DISRUPTION POTENTIAL: 8.0

THE DOMINANCE OF DATA

As we saw in the chapter on second screen, one of the promises of the new age of television is the dominance of data that's used for the good of all the relevant parties: content owners, content holders, and consumers alike. How this actually plays out will depend on the continued good faith efforts of all parties not to take advantage of the data for their own selfish means.

The underpinning of this data revolution is the notion that all users will soon have individual accounts, much in the way that they currently have individual mobile phone accounts. This will allow whoever is collecting the data to know who within a household is watching what show, clicking (or not fast-forwarding) on which commercial, and other nuggets that were heretofore unknown when we only had access to household information.

So, for instance, thanks to data, the system would know that the 18-year-old daughter in the house was watching *Glee*, and would thus not serve her ads for men's razors or "cover the gray" hair dyes. And since it would know that she'd sat through a few commercials for the Gap, it would offer her up as the target for an H&M ad based on her prior behavior. The more she watched, the more the system would learn about her, including the types of shows she watched and when and how she watched them. That would allow the system to provide her with better recommendations and would provide the programming department with insights into the types of shows favored by young women in her demographic.

The ultimate goal, the holy grail, is to create a system where there are fewer, more highly targeted commercials. Since these commercials will reach a much more relevant audience, they'll fetch more money and thus there will be no drop in overall revenue.

Or something like that.

The data gleaned from digital systems that track a user's every move has been able to impact (if not fully disrupt) a range of industries from retail to print media. TV, with its Nielsen households, has been resistant thus far, but it seems to be only a matter of time before big data disrupts the Television Industrial Complex as well.

Netflix has been a key proponent of the use of data, though it should be pointed out that their use cases are mostly hearsay—as a subscription-only service, Netflix does not have to put out actual viewership numbers, and doesn't. So when Netflix says they used data analysis to choose a political drama like *House of Cards*, as the data indicated it would be popular with their audience, we have no reason to disbelieve them. *House of Cards* certainly generated a lot of buzz, and we can assume, a goodly sized audience. It's just not readily quantifiable—they have not pulled back the curtain and let anyone see the actual numbers.

MAXIMUM METADATA

Metadata is another area where Netflix has taken the lead, though perhaps inadvertently. In order to properly sort out their movie catalog into quirky subcategories like "Dark Movies Starring Independent Women" the network hired a few hundred people whose job was to watch every movie in the catalog and tag them with terms that went beyond the usual comedy/drama/family positioning. As a result, Netflix has much richer metadata (tags that describe a piece of content for search and recommendation engines) than anyone else in the industry. They are able to parse those tags to spot trends and patterns in consumption that help inform both their content creation and content acquisition choices.

In addition, the rich metadata helps improve Netflix recommendations for existing viewers.

Social media is another rich source of data. Several companies have arisen (and been funded) whose goal is to help both content owners and advertisers better understand who their audiences are and what plot points or scenes create social media buzz. This is a tricky argument however, as most social media monitoring involves scraping Twitter—Facebook posts are by and large private— and as discussed previously, Twitter is a niche product used by a niche audience. So many people—myself included—remain skeptical of the overall accuracy of social media stats on their own. Cross-referencing those stats with stats about tune-in and demographics can be valuable, however, and so it would be unwise to dismiss them out of hand.

One interesting use of data comes from a Palo Alto-based company called Boxfish. Boxfish collects the closed captioning that's required for every U.S. TV show and uses it to determine what terms and phrases are currently trending. The company provides more long-term analysis as well.

"Compared to the digital space, TV data is relatively thin," says Eoin Dowling, Boxfish's founder. "Discovery, navigation, and monetization hinge off a program title and demographic. Try to find content on TV around Lebron James and you will struggle. Google, Twitter, and Facebook do a great job of delivering content that is real-time and interest based This is what Boxfish is delivering to the ecosystem. A real-time layer of data that provides discovery and monetization based on what the user is interested in."

The flip side of Big Data is privacy concerns. Viewers don't necessarily want their every move exposed, even it if it anonymized. There's a very Big Brother-ish aspect to the notion that every click and pause and fast-forward is being recorded in some giant database to be used for the benefit of some faceless corporation. There's also the sense that Big Data doesn't always get it right.

The poster child for Big Data gone awry is a 2001 Wall Street Journal article entitled *My TiVo Thinks I'm Gay* about a reporter whose young niece had watched a few days' worth of tween girl programming and whose TiVo then sent him female-oriented recommendations (funny how homophobic that headline sounds fourteen years later. But I digress.)

Even today, there is a sense that most recommendation services don't get it right. Piksel did a survey in December 2013 and 43% of the respondents whose MVPD had a recommendation engine reported that they did not "find it useful at all."

Social recommendations are another area that gets a lot of buzz (and VC dollars) but may be of limited value. Our social graphs often consist of people who do not share our tastes—elderly aunts, the kid who sat next to you in third grade—and surfacing their choices does not make for an effective recommendation system. Going back to that same Piksel survey, only 10% of respondents expressed a strong interest in seeing recommendations from their social graph.

When I mention this to people with a vested interest in those systems, the response I inevitably get is, "we can tweak the system to allow users to specify which friends they want to include and which they want to eliminate." Which sounds great in theory, but in practice, how many people are actually going to want to go through their list of 500+ Facebook friends to rank them?

Hardly any.

Viewers don't want to do any work in order to help boost the accuracy of their recommendations. Or most of them, anyway. This means that things like asking viewers to select their favorite channels (out of a line-up of 1800 options) are doomed from the start. People want their apps to work—they don't want to do work for the apps.

There's also the problem of linear channels and sorting "what's on right now" from "what could you be watching given what you have on VOD and on your DVR?" If you're an MVPD, you want to drive live tune-in, so your system needs to be biased in that direction. Pure OTT players like Netflix and Hulu don't have to worry about that. Everything is always on. And so their recommendations can serve as their version of the EPG, surfacing shows and categories you might be interested in and helping you to wade through the thousands of programs available to you.

The same algorithms that power recommendation engines can be put into play to serve up the most relevant advertising. They'll learn consumer preferences based on what shows they watch, which commercials they watch, which ones they skip, and (if we really want to throw privacy concerns out the window) what they've bought on their credit card.

The result, as mentioned previously, of analyzing all that data would be a system with fewer, better targeted commercials. Putting a commercial in front of people who are likely to find the message relevant should be worth more to advertisers, the theory goes, since they are only reaching those people who are likely to watch it and respond to it.

Everyone has bought into this bright new future, with one exception: the advertisers themselves. They don't want to reach narrowly targeted audiences. They want to reach a broader audience to increase "branding"—i.e., the perception the brand has in the world at large. They do this to ensure they have a steady pipeline of new customers and to increase the perceived value of the brand. (Mercedes doesn't only want to reach people with the resources to buy a $70,000 vehicle. They want to reach people who might know somebody with the resources to buy a $70,000 vehicle, so that when their brother-in-law shows up one day with a new Mercedes, they'll be impressed that he's been able to buy such a high-class car.)

Without having advertisers come on board, this whole system falls apart. Which is why it will be crucial, over the next few years, to be able to prove the value of this sort of targeted advertising, to show advertisers and their media buying agencies that highly targeted ads are a better value than scattershot ads. Though given the amorphous nature of advertising (did the ad contribute to the sale or did the placement on the shelf, the color of the logo, or some combination of all three?) "proof" is going to require as much a leap of faith as anything else.

Data can play a big role in programming decisions as well, pointing out the types of shows that appeal to certain audiences and letting networks make better decisions on what to green light.

Or not.

Programming is arguably an art, not a science, and while Netflix's data showed that their viewers would be interested in seeing a political drama, *House of Cards* succeeded because it was a well done show—not because it was a political drama. The latter fact is icing on the cake and probably allowed it to find a bigger audience on Netflix, but a different political drama, one that was not as well crafted, would likely have sunk.

While that sounds obvious, I'm often surprised how many people seem to feel that data operates in a vacuum, that things like quality and entertainment value are mere add-ons, nice-to-haves.

They're not.

Data, and the ability to track individual viewers across devices (and perhaps beyond) is definitely a force for disruption in the industry. How much of a force will depend on how wisely it is deployed.

SUMMARY

As television becomes completely digital, there's a treasure trove of data around consumers' viewing and spending habits. This data can be used to make better programming decisions and to make sure the right ads reach the right audiences.

DISRUPTION POTENTIAL: 9

CORD CUTTING

One of the easiest ways to get clicks on a tech-oriented blog these days is to run an article about the death of television. It's something the Silicon Valley crowd has been waiting for (along with the Apple TV) since the disruption of the music industry fifteen years ago.

But dig a little deeper, past the comments from gloaters and satisfied cord cutters, and chances are what you'll find is a prediction based on a small-scale study done by a research company smart enough to realize that death-of-TV studies get a lot of pick-up.

Because the fact is that cord cutting isn't really happening. At least not yet.

Before we go into why, let's put a few definitions out there: "Cord cutting" is what happens when someone who previously had both a broadband and pay-TV subscription decides to terminate the pay-TV subscription and rely on some combination of over the top (OTT) services like Netflix and Amazon, free web video and over-the-air signals. It's often viewed as a moral decision of sorts, done by someone who can easily afford pay TV but who feels they are sending a message about its high costs and lack of quality. Cord cutters, who are definitely riding a wave of artisanal Brooklyn-style cool, are in many ways the descendants of people who bragged about not owning a TV back in the 70s and 80s. Or not. There's a school of thought that says most cord cutters are doing it for economic reasons and plan to re-up once their economic fortunes improve.

Variations on "cord cutters" are "cord nevers," "cord shavers," and "cord plussers."

"Cord Nevers" are people, generally recent graduates, who have never had a pay TV subscription and don't see the need for one. It's never been clear how much of that is a moral decision, how much is an economic one, and how much is just the fact that unmarried 25-year-olds aren't home enough to actually watch TV. Cord Nevers scare the TV Industrial Complex because they seem to indicate a trend—millennials don't see the need for pay television. Which is quite possible. Though it's equally possible (perhaps even more so) that when this generation settles down, has kids, and buys their house in the suburbs, they'll decide pay TV is a really good idea, whatever pay TV looks like at that point. (Note too that a lot of those studies of millennials seem not to take into account that many 18- to 24-year-olds still live at home, in a college dorm, or with roommates who may have the pay-TV account in their names.)

"Cord Shavers" are people who have, largely for economic reasons, cut back on services they once had, like HBO or multiple set-top boxes. Their growth seems largely attributable to the recent Great Recession and motivated by a desire to save money. Some have seen this (largely anecdotal) trend as evidence that consumers are pushing back on the price they pay for TV service—that the operators have reached their saturation point—but it may just be the value of those extra services and channels rather than the value of the entire system. Regardless, I have yet to see any stats showing it's becoming an actual phenomenon.

"Cord Plussers" are those at the other end of the spectrum, people who already have the titanium pay-TV package but are adding on OTT services like Netflix, Hulu, and Amazon. There are some numbers to support this: Netflix indexes much higher with affluent consumers (with pay TV subscriptions) than it does with poor ones. It's also common sense, to a degree: given Netflix's low cost ($8.99/month), why wouldn't you add it on to your existing service? If you're paying $150/month to light up premium service on three or four TVs, $8.99 sounds like a bargain.

So back to cord cutting. Here's the deal: pay TV in the U.S. has a close to 90% penetration rate. We were at around 80% penetration at the turn of the millennium, then satellite TV, which reached parts of the country wire-based cable couldn't, helped push that number north of 85% where its remained ever since.

Cord-cutting believers (or fantasists, the choice of nomenclature is yours) often cite the fact that the number of pay-TV subscribers fell during seven of the eight quarters prior to Q2 2014. Which is a true stat. Unfortunately (for their argument, anyway) the net effect of all that cord cutting was that the pay-TV industry lost 0.2% of its subscribers during that time.

Now if you're looking for clicks, 0.2% is actually something like 300,000 people. So the raw numbers look pretty ominous. It's only when you do the math that you realize how insignificant they are, particularly when you look at the reason why. Noted Wall Street analyst Craig Moffett attributes much of that cord cutting to economic necessity and believes that unlike the "moral" cord cutters we discussed earlier, "economic" cord cutters are just as likely to return to the fold once their finances improve. TV is often the last thing people give up when times get hard, and so it makes sense that it's one of the first things they restore when they regain liquidity.

"One of the most overhyped memes of the recent past is the so-called 'Death of Television'," says Robert Tercek, a former MTV executive who is one of the industry's most highly sought-after consultants, for both startups and traditional TV companies. "This phrase has reverberated throughout the blogosphere despite the fact that there is zero evidence to support it. The phrase is nothing more than Exhibit A of typical wishful thinking by tech-obsessed pundits who worship at the altar of disruption. At a time when television is robust and growing, with advertising revenue, total audience size, and subscriber numbers all rising, it seems quite obvious that reports about the death of television have been greatly exaggerated."

One of the things that seems to be stopping people from actually cutting the cord is the lack of viable alternatives. While it's possible to string together a system from over-the-air signals, Netflix, Hulu and similar services, the resulting service is definitely sub-optimal: there's a lot of switching back and forth between inputs, a lot of waiting as you move from one platform to another, no ability to channel surf, and few options for just having the TV as background noise. For someone who rarely watches television, this is a fine solution, but for a moderate to heavy viewer, it feels like a serious compromise.

What's important to remember is that while cord cutting may not be an issue today, that doesn't mean it's an empty threat.

If the TV industry does absolutely nothing to improve the user experience and continues to raise prices without offering less expensive alternatives, then cord cutting will become a reality, and as more users make the break, the cord-free experience itself will become far more user-friendly as more companies rush in to fill the void. "This situation would create a big opportunity for scrappy startup companies who have nothing to lose," notes Tercek. "The startup ventures will compete fiercely, and the winners will emerge with an entirely new skill set and programming model that is optimized for the new economics of digital distribution."

Right now, a complete meltdown of the TV Industrial Complex seems unlikely to happen. While people are watching much less live TV than ever, they're still watching pay TV via DVR and VOD. The trend towards OTT—networks setting up their own apps and marketing them directly to consumers as MVPDs struggle with TV Everywhere—is notable, but in the end all it does is move costs from one place to another and many observers point out that a system of a dozen or so network OTT apps may actually be more expensive than a current MVPD package with hundreds of channels to choose from.

There's also a bigger issue with cord cutting: the same company that owns the pay TV cord also owns the broadband cord. So cut your Comcast TV service and you're still paying Comcast for broadband. That gives those companies incredible leverage and as we saw in earlier chapters, most people don't have much of a choice when it comes to broadband providers.

But if cord cutting does become more prevalent, the MVPDs aren't going to be the ones who get hurt: they'll just rejigger their pricing so that you're paying for all that extra bandwidth you're using to stream Netflix. They may even team up with the networks to offer you "broadband only" packages that do away with the set-top box (MVPDs generally hate set-top boxes) and give you five or ten OTT channels as part of your monthly charge.

In other words, they are not going to be losing any money.

The industry, at some level, understands (or is beginning to understand) that the future can't be ignored, that millennials do have different viewing habits, that they've passed these habits on to their parents and grandparents, and that things like user experience really do matter. How and when the industry solves this is another story, but as we'll see in upcoming chapters, many of these "fixes" are already in the works.

SUMMARY

Cord Cutting does not seem to be a real threat just yet. But given how many people report thinking about cutting the cord, it's something the TV Industrial Complex should take note of.

Or not. The MVPDs currently own both the pay-TV and the internet connections in most households. The MVPDs would be able to get around cord-cutting by shifting costs, but the networks would lose ad revenue.

DISRUPTION POTENTIAL: 9.5

SECTION 3

Future Predictions

TV EVERYWHERE

This is the fun part, where I get to predict the future based on what's going on today, what I've learned during years of working in the industry, and my thoughts on what it is that consumers want and don't want.

It's not an exact science by any means and every day something new happens to move my view of the future in one direction or another. But I think the basics still hold.

The first thing I see becoming a reality is TV Everywhere (TVE), which is basically what you have now if you have Netflix: you can watch your pay TV service on any device at any time. If you've paused a show on your iPad and want to resume it on the TV, you can do that seamlessly.

The technology is there to make this happen, save one crucial part: the ability to measure ratings on various devices, which would allow the networks to keep the same ad revenue. It's something the industry has been waiting on for a while now, ever since it was first announced that Nielsen was trying to make it happen back in February 2013. And while there have been hints and updates that progress was being made—including an October 2014 announcement that Nielsen was working with Adobe to make online ratings happen, nothing final has been released as of March 2015.

That's why so many MVPDs are holding back on their current

TVE offerings. A study conducted by Digitalsmiths in early 2014 revealed that more than half of their respondents were unaware that their provider even had a TVE app, although Comcast recently reported that 30% of their customers are regular users of their Xfinity TV Go TVE app, which has 11 million downloads.

There are two possible options for TV Everywhere: a system where the MVPDs proprietary TV Everywhere apps prevail, or one where the networks proprietary OTT apps do.

I'm betting on the former, and here's why.

A BUILT-IN AUDIENCE OF MILLIONS. Any new OTT service, whether it's a skinny bundle like Sling TV or a network app like HBO Now, must first build an audience from scratch. The MVPD's however, already have a huge built-in audience for their apps: the millions of people who are already paying for their service. All the MVPDs have to do is convince them to download a free TVE app and start using it. There's nothing to give up, nothing to replace, and (most notably) nothing to pay for. That's an incredibly strong selling point.

ALL THOSE AD DOLLARS. Thanks to this built-in potential audience of millions, selling ads on the operator TVE apps will be much easier when compared to other OTT TV apps. As the networks start to see the ad revenue flow in, they'll become less resistant to the idea of striking deals to put their shows on the operator apps. They may even go crazy and allow viewers to have access to their home DVR or VOD systems through these apps. Stranger things have happened.

EASE OF USE. Because operator TVE apps are integrated into the user's existing pay-TV system, they (theoretically) should be easier to set up. For instance, the app should (again, theoretically) automatically log on to the home WiFi system, since the user is already registered and the Time Warner app, once set up, can recognize that the user is a Time Warner TV customer.

Then there's the fact that there are dozens of channels, all at no additional cost, and you can flip from one to another with minimal hassle. That's a major advantage, because when you're dealing with a dozen or so standalone apps, switching from one channel to another most definitely becomes a *major* hassle.

Operator TVE apps also let you easily move between *all* devices. So when your brother gives up his spot in front of the 72-

inch home theater in the den, you can slide right in, push the Patriots game from your iPad to the TV set, and you'll be sitting pretty in seconds. That's the advantage of having a TVE service that's also connected to your set-top box.

(Never underestimate the power of convenience: remember how the MVPDs were able to beat TiVo at the DVR game by offering up their own versions, built right into the same set-top box the consumer was already leasing from them. The functionality on those DVRs was horrible when compared to TiVo, but it was also practically free, the cable tech installed it for you, and if it broke it was the MVPDs problem not yours. Look for a similar reaction with the TVE apps; the MVPDs might not have the best apps and the best interfaces, but they're way more convenient.)

THE MVPDS CONTROL THE INTERNET (OR AT LEAST THE LAST MILE). Because MVPDs are also broadband network owners, they get to make the rules. Rules like "if you really want the broadband-only package, we can sell it to you, but for five dollars more we can throw in our basic pay-television package with 35 channels and a free TV Everywhere app." That's a difficult offer to resist, no matter how much of an Apple fan-boy you might be.

And as operator TVE apps get more popular and families start streaming hours of video, families who are MVPD customers won't be looking at draconian bandwidth caps, since unlimited high-speed bandwidth will be part of their 'titanium' double- or triple-play package.

On the other hand, while MVPDs are in a great position with respect to OTT, It's not all free sledding from here. MVPDs are notoriously bad at user interfaces (we'll talk about interfaces in the chapter on "BYOD") and if their TVE app is torturous to use, then the millions of potential viewers will not use the app. Similarly, if the MVPDs and networks fail to give users access to TV content from VOD or DVR (or both), then that's a big minus (though the "free" part of "free TVE app" is always going to be very compelling).

So give it time. As things change, the networks will realize that it's in their best interests to be part of a user-friendly guide. Even if the industry goes 100% OTT, the MVPDs aren't going anywhere: they control the internet. Or at least your access to it.

PERSONALIZATION

One key to creating better recommendations—and better ad targeting—is to give users individual accounts. This will be a coup for the television industry, which has jealously been watching as their cousins, the telecom industry, have taken America from one-landline per household to one-landline and four cell phones per household. And everything that means in terms of increased ARPU (average revenue per user) and being able to better target both customers and advertising.

Personalization will likely start off the way Netflix currently has it, by asking you to log in to your personal account from the home screen. If you're on a personal device, like an iPad, it will likely keep you logged in. Future versions will rely on things like facial recognition or fingerprint scanning. (The challenge with facial recognition is finding a way to make it seem less creepy.)

Your personalized account will also mean that you will receive advertising that is specifically targeted to you, based on your tastes and interests, even your recent credit card activity. (That would have to be opt-in.) You'll see fewer, better targeted commercials too. While advertisers currently have a tough time with that, preferring broad-based targeting that encourages brand awareness, I feel confident a happy medium can be reached so that people who fall into the "maybe interested" or even "maybe knows someone who might be interested" categories will be included in branding efforts.

It's important that advertisers understand that it's going to be increasingly harder for a generation raised on Netflix and iTunes to go back to a model that relies on four- or five-minute commercial blocks. They're just not going to take it and will seek out alternate means (pirating, cloud DVRs) of viewing to avoid painfully long commercial breaks. But give them shorter, more relevant blocks, throw in a timer to show just how many seconds they've got to run to the kitchen and back, and there's a good chance they'll accept it and maybe even watch it.

IN-HOME VERSUS OUT-OF-HOME

We will see in-home TV Everywhere long before we see it extended out of home. Part of that is due to the fact that it's easier to authenticate users whose WiFi comes from the same provider as their pay-TV service. That's sort of a no-brainer. But there's also the use case scenario: other than live sporting events and breaking news stories, there aren't that many instances I can think of where people would want to watch TV outside their homes. I mean it's not like you're going to head down to Starbucks with your iPad to watch an episode of *Game of Thrones,* when you can watch it at home on your 65-inch HDTV.

Travel is a possibility, but the world of frequent business travelers is a small one and setting up a system to service people for one or two weeks a year doesn't seem worth it. What would make sense for travelers is a system that allows them to save a show for future viewing (a sort of portable DVR) so they don't need to worry about WiFi or 4G connections, but that's a feature, not a platform.

Train commuters (and I am part of that demographic) might appreciate the ability to watch TV on the go, but first they'll need WiFi and/or cellular service to catch up with them. Moving from tower to tower does not an optimum viewing experience make.

I had one vendor of out-of-home TV service tell me that the office was a likely use case, but there again, all I could wonder was "Where do you work?" because historic events like presidential inaugurations and night janitors aside, I could not remember it ever being okay to watch TV at the office.

In-home also makes sense from a practicality point of view. It may not make sense to keep a television in the sun room or upstairs guest room, but an iPad or 21-inch monitor makes an excellent TV substitute on the rare occasions someone might want to be there.

There are also rights issues around allowing in-home and out-of-home viewing (negotiating in-home rights is easier than out-of-home) and the perception that it's easier for viewers to act on an ad when they are at home rather than on the road.

So there's our first prediction: in-home TV Everywhere will happen before out-of-home.

THAT TWENTY-FIRST CENTURY FEELING

One of the key things that fully functioning TV Everywhere will provide is the sense that TV has finally caught up with every other media and entered the twenty-first century. Because right now, every time you turn on your set-top box it still feels like 1994. That's particularly exacerbated by the fact that the alternatives, OTT services like Netflix and Hulu, feel like 2015. Being able to access TV from any device will also free it from the television set and make it a more personal medium. Meaning that watching TV was always somewhat public— anyone walking into the room could see what you were watching, but with an iPad or similar tablet device, the viewing experience becomes much more private and thus more personal.

This may actually help the growth of niche content as people begin to see video as their personal library and become more willing to branch out with their tastes. Someone watching TV on an iPad with headphones on is not watching as background noise: they're concentrating on what they're watching and are involved in their show. The ability to watch what we want and when takes away some of the serendipity of channel surfing, but it also gives us the go-ahead to demand quality from TV programming, something that wasn't always available in the past when we were limited to whatever was on linear TV. Watching on a personal device also gives us a personal connection to the story: we are shut off from the world and alone with the characters. That's a far richer and more intense scenario than sitting in the living room reading the newspaper and chatting while the TV blares constantly in the background.

UNBUNDLING

One consequence of TV Everywhere may be the start of unbundling, of not allowing network groups to demand that every channel they own be included in the line-up. Viewers may be offered a slimmed-down TV Everywhere package where they get to choose 200 or 400 channels for their devices. (There will be no need for SD channels, which immediately cuts the number of available channels down considerably.) There is a strong argument that unbundling will only result in fewer channels and higher prices, but by allowing for smaller bouquets (industry terminology for a grouping of channels) exclusively on connected devices, we may be able to have our cake and eat it too: the network groups will still be able to keep their bundles and get paid for them, but consumers will be able to get a more personalized line-up on their tablets and smartphones.

This is likely to be the case even if the networks all go rogue and start selling directly to consumers: in order to keep their smaller channels happy, they'll start including them in their bundles.

DOWNLOADING

The final piece of the TV Everywhere puzzle will be the ability to download shows to watch later on our personal devices. This should solve the out-of-home dilemma for most people as it will allow viewers to stop and pick up where they left off, something that should prove useful on a commute. (Few things are as frustrating as getting to your final destination with five minutes left to watch on a linear broadcast show.) Downloadable content will also allow viewers to watch content on their own schedules, the way they would with VOD or a DVR. It would also solve the legal dilemma presented by the current state of U.S. copyright law, which insists that operators create individual copies of shows for DVR-style viewing (versus a single copy in the cloud that every viewer is able to download.) Allowing phones and tablets to serve as DVRs makes the entire TV Everywhere experience even more useful to viewers, especially if we go back to the original paradigm of purposeful versus non-purposeful viewing: given the solitary nature of the experience, people are much more likely to purposefully pull out a tablet to watch a favorite show than they are to just watch it as background noise while doing something else.

Dish, the U.S. satellite provider, already has this functionality built into their DISH Anywhere app and it has proven to be a popular feature for all the reasons listed above. Dish, whose CEO, Charlie Ergen, has a reputation for being a maverick in an industry known for its conservatism, has introduced a number of forward-thinking features such as a tablet-based program guide with social functionality and the ability to watch programming remotely utilizing the Sling technology Ergen purchased in 2007. (Sling, which makes the Slingbox devices as well as the Dish SlingHopper, basically mirrors the user's set-top box on a PC or mobile device so that when you change a channel on the Slingbox, the channel is actually changed on the set-top box. When Slingboxes were limited to a small cadre of road warriors who wanted to be able to watch TV from their hotel rooms, the networks did not deem it enough of an issue to warrant the attention of their legal teams.)

MISSION CRITICAL

Solving the TV Everywhere equation is crucial for the MVPDs as it will allow them to maintain their control over the TV viewing population by providing a clear indication of how they're adapting to the 21st century and both meeting and matching the expectations set by Netflix and other OTT providers. Consumers don't see TVE as a nice-to-have option but rather as table stakes—doubly true for younger millennials who have grown up with Netflix and don't remember a world without it.

I think most if not all of the MVPDs will make this happen as the networks realize it's the best way for them to maintain something resembling the current ecosystem and the cash flow that comes along with it. The alternative—a series of network apps that allow for a direct relationship with the consumer may sound good on paper, but will only create a confusing and somewhat chaotic landscape that makes discovering new content harder and solidifies power in the hands of a few larger networks or network groups. Say what you will about the MVPDs, the current system gives viewers an easier path for discovering new and niche content by aggregating it all into one place and by providing a universal discovery mechanism. It's the way to create a win both for consumers and for content creators of all sizes.

THE FUTURE OF SECOND SCREEN

Second screen interactions will continue to proliferate and become an integral part of the TV landscape. Social TV interactions will become common on live events, sporting events, and reality game shows. Scripted series will have second screen experiences that feel more like DVD extras: interviews with cast and crew, behind-the-scenes looks, quizzes, polls, and message boards. These second screen and social experiences will also create an advertising market as brands can use them to interact with hardcore fans of a show.

I've often felt that "second screen" was the wrong word to describe the types of experiences that we'll see in the future. It somehow implies that people will be looking manically from screen to screen, trying to keep track of where they should be focused.

But nothing could be farther from the truth.

Dual-screen apps rarely work. They're good for game shows where the audience can use them to play along. Or for sporting events, where stats and replays are available to look at during the frequent breaks in the action.

Otherwise, no one really wants to interact when they're watching TV. The late John Gardner once described reading fiction as a "vivid and continuous dream." The same goes for well-crafted television. You are in a world with the characters and you don't want to be jerked out of it. That's why commercials can be so jarring: they snap us out of the dream world.

Where second screen or additional content works best for most types of programming is after the show is over. And it only works for viewers who are serious fans of the show. Those are the people who are happy to extend the experience. Who are glad when they're able to spend more time with the characters, the actors, the writers, and the producers. Not to mention the other serious fans.

What's going to be tricky is finding the right sorts of experiences that will get them to stay rather than go out and create their own experiences (something that happens quite often, as we saw in the chapter on fan communities). That balance will be different for every show. Some will rely exclusively on stories, others on stats, shopping, and even social media. It will all really depend on the content of the show and what the hardcore fans are most interested in seeing.

The post-show additional content will in many ways resemble DVD extras and the smarter showrunners will create enough additional content for their hardcore fans to also create an opportunity for advertisers. The additional content sites can be sponsored by brands that want to reach the fan base. Or they can run advertising, either pre-roll video ads or static banners, depending on what the fan base will bear. Product placement is also an option. What this does is open up an additional door for monetization as well as a way to keep fans engaged between seasons and beyond.

As we discussed in the chapter on fan communities, many popular shows continue to live on and find new fans as the years go on. Additional content sites make it easy for newcomers to find the communities they're looking for and to interact with each other and have a deeper and more enriching experience around the show. For many shows, the fan communities will live off site on fan-run sites and it will be up to the showrunners to make deals with them to port some of the content onto the official show site. For other shows, letting fans run their own sites and message boards will make more sense. (There's nothing sadder than a lonely message board.) Fan fiction, whether contests or links, can also be incorporated into the additional content experience. Or not. It will depend on the relationship established between the showrunners and the fan base. But new fans will find it, either way.

Once shows are released overseas, additional content can either be separated by language or combined to create a more cosmopolitan community, allowing U.S. and overseas fans to cross-pollinate.

SOCIAL MEDIA

While I see a lot of opportunities for production companies to create experiences around their shows, I'm less optimistic about the chances of Facebook and (especially) Twitter to become a part of this future ecosystem, mostly because I believe their role lies in driving tune-in via paid posts and tweets.

The truth is few people are all that interested in what random strangers have to say on Twitter or Facebook. Particularly because what those strangers have to say is rarely very interesting.

What they do want to hear, though, is what celebrities or media figures have to say. That's far more interesting and also far more likely to be surfaced via one of Twitter's new "tweet ads" that live on third-party sites. Tweet ads can be anything from promos from the networks, live tweets from the cast during the show, to tweets from well known characters and should become a huge tune-in driver. Especially now that Twitter is allowing up to 30 seconds of native video. This means networks can send out clips, full-on promos or other video content along with a 140-character call to action in a package that doesn't really look like an ad. Once program guide apps are hooked up to the social platforms, viewers should be able to click on a tweet to either tune-in or mark a program for later viewing.

Facebook's value, like Twitter's, will be in its role as a promotional vehicle for the networks. Facebook video ads can be slotted to run in the news feeds of anyone who fits the demographic profile of a show or who has liked that show or something similar. Given the size of Facebook's audience, it should prove invaluable for, say, ABC to be able to send out a teaser ad an hour before *Scandal* airs, especially since users should be able to log into their MVPD accounts with Facebook and tune in.

The number of people who'll actively engage on the various social media is finite. That has to do with psychology more than anything: most people aren't wired to share their thoughts on television shows with random strangers, even on Facebook where the strangers are less random. That includes liking and sharing, which have a higher threshold, but a threshold nonetheless.

The number of people who'll view tweets and posts and snaps about TV shows is fairly infinite, and that's where the power of social media lies: to provide a non-interruptive promotional vehicle for television programming that reaches a fairly infinite pool of potential viewers.

WHERE THE SECOND SCREEN EXPERIENCE LIVES

One of the problems behind the adoption of second screen apps has been the fact that they are indeed apps and need to be downloaded individually. Most of them could not be used to control the set-top box, making discovery something of a chore as the viewer had to put down the app, pick up the remote and change the channel, then revert back to the app.

This was not a good system for many reasons, one of the main ones being that users already had too many apps and were in no way interested in downloading yet another one, particularly one that had no discernible functionality.

That's why I believe that the second screen experience of the not-too-distant future will be launched off of a tablet-based program guide. It will be an option that you can call up at any point, though I suspect for most shows, that point will be once the show is over. It will take you into a very immersive experience and return you back to the program guide. So there won't be any extra apps to download, nothing to search for, nothing to lose track of. The app will be the same across all MVPD systems (provided we still get our TV from MVPDs, which I suspect we will) and the fact that these experiences are universal will allow national advertisers to come on board since they can now count on larger numbers and treat second screen like a real medium rather than an experiment.

For things like reality game shows and quiz shows, a lot of the current crop of while-you're-watching polls and quizzes will play an important part, but for scripted programs, the app will be more about deeper fan engagement. And that will be the beauty of the system and why we will accept it: because whatever the experience is, it will feel like an organic extension of the show itself and not some bolted on "second screen experience" or "social TV engagement." And the more organic the experience feels, the more popular it will become. Which will involve a shift in expectations, from creating something an advertiser would value to something a fan would value. But once that shift is made, the fans will come, and the advertisers will value the result even more. There's a line there—the experiences can't become too commercial, too crass—or fans will flee for something of their own creation. And that line will vary depending on the type of show: what reality show fans might regard as acceptable, fans of a teen drama might recoil from. As always, it all comes down to knowing your audience.

MONETIZING THE SECOND SCREEN

The appeal of second screen—and why it creates a gleam in the eyes of VCs and network executives alike—is its potential for monetization. Because rather than just giving away all that additional content for free, there's the chance to get someone else to pay for it.

That's why so many of the early second screen experiences were designed with advertisers in mind. The easier it was to express the results of the experiment to the CMO as a PDF, the better. *Forty thousand people interacted with Acme Corp's commercial, of which 25,000 downloaded the companion app and 15,000 downloaded the coupon and 10,000 redeemed the coupon...* that's the stuff marketing dreams are made of. Unfortunately, those interactions don't carry a lot of weight with consumers, who see them as just another way to save a few dollars, not a reason to bond with the show that's hosting the interaction.

That's why the data play I spoke about in the last section is going to be so valuable: the more networks and social platforms know about a viewer and the shows and brands they like, the more valuable that viewer becomes. As viewers begin to use their social media credentials to authenticate their MVPD log-ins, the industry gathers even more data about them.

That's not necessarily a bad thing, though. Privacy advocates to the contrary, the plus side to all this data is a better, more customized experience, where the shows recommended to you are the ones you actually want to see and the ads that show up are for products you might actually want to buy. It won't happen overnight, but eventually the system should work to help you sort your way through the morass of available options while still leaving room for serendipitous discovery. The specifics of how that happens are for those with far more mathematical brains to figure out, but a system that consistently surfaces options the viewer regards favorably would seem to be in everyone's interest.

We just have to hope the powers that be don't get too greedy.

BYOD (BRING YOUR OWN DEVICE)

Few things frustrate the MVPDs the way set-top boxes do. They are expensive, often unreliable, not particularly consumer friendly, and lack any sense of style. Worse still, they need to be installed, which costs the MVPD a few hundred dollars every time they have to roll out a truck. Cable installers are notoriously unreliable, and that leads to frustrated customers who've taken off the morning from work and are taking to Twitter, Facebook, and more analog options to complain. On more than one occasion I've heard MVPD executives complain that the boxes and their installation process are "why people hate us."

Which is another problem: every year when surveys of the "most hated companies in America" are conducted, several of the MPVDs wind up in the top 10—for many reasons, but the unreliability of their set-top boxes certainly doesn't help.

It got so bad that Comcast set up one of the early social media success stories, empowering Frank Eliason and his team to use the Twitter account @comcastcares to try and accommodate Twitter users who were complaining about their service or (usually) about their installer not showing up. And while Eliason's team did some good and staunched the spread of the #ComcastSucks hashtag, they could only provide a band-aid, and not a very sturdy one at that, as recent customer service scandals continue to paint Comcast in a very negative light, possibly impacting their upcoming merger with Time-Warner.

That's why most pay-TV providers are looking at another solution, which they've named "BYOD" or "Bring Your Own Device"—getting consumers to supply their own set-top boxes or the equivalents thereof. It makes a lot of sense, actually, when you consider that these devices are all under $100 and provide a better user experience. They also allow the user to access all their streaming services from the same device without having to do the dreaded input switch, which often involves searching for the original TV remote before returning to the set-top box remote.

The idea would be to provide an app for Roku, Apple TV, Amazon Fire, Chromecast et al. that would play the MVPDs' live streams and VOD along with some sort of cloud-based DVR. (Or not—as we'll see, the DVR may not figure in the MVPDs future plans if everything becomes available on VOD.) Users would also have the option of downloading a tablet app that worked to control an internet enabled TV, using the home WiFi network. It's also possible that MVPDs would sell a branded Roku or Chromecast, available either via mail or at local electronics stores, that came preloaded with their program guide as the default menu.

There are many advantages to this sort of set-up, first and foremost among them the fact that streaming devices are much smaller than old school set-top boxes (the largest are about the size of a hockey puck and Roku's and Chromecast's are available as thumb drive-sized "sticks") They also allow for much more user-friendly interfaces. They're easily updated (or replaced, given the low cost), updates can be automatically pushed out over the internet, and no one needs to come to the house to install them.

The gamble is that consumers will get wise to the fact that the MVPDs are now pushing the responsibility of obtaining a set-top box off on them, but my assumption is that people will be so happy at the prospect of losing their clunky old boxes that they won't mind.

The tablet and smartphone will also play a role in this ecosystem, serving as remote controls and program guides for both internet-enabled TVs and streaming devices. Providers may even start to give away 8-inch mini-tablets to use exclusively as program guide/remote controls. That seems to be the ideal size in that it allows for a decent amount of the guide to be seen in a single screen, without taking up its own seat on the sofa the way a full sized tablet might.

Mini-tablets have keyboards, which helps make searching easier, and they also have enough storage that viewers can use them to download shows for offline viewing. Everyone in the family will have their own tablet/remote which is synced to their personal account. When two or more family members (or friends) are watching together, their accounts will talk to each other and determine what the best joint viewing options are and which commercials are best suited to the group.

Voice commands will also be a part of this new world. Rather than type in the names of shows, viewers will be able to search by speaking the names of what they want to watch. As the systems get more sophisticated, they'll allow for more generalized searches ("I want to see a romantic movie with my husband tonight") and as metadata becomes more sophisticated, they'll be able to search based on fragments rather than full titles ("Show me the episode of *Big Bang Theory* where Leonard's mother comes to visit"). The more people use these sophisticated remotes, the more the underlying system will learn about them to the point of being able to predict and anticipate their choices.

Old school remote controls won't disappear either—they'll just get smaller and more streamlined, sort of the way the current Roku and Apple TV remotes look today with just a few simple buttons. Not everyone will want to use them, but they'll always be an option, particularly for older viewers who are not 100% comfortable with the tablet experience.

The tablets will also open up an additional screen, programmed in most cases by the network, that can be used for a variety of purposes while the viewer is watching TV. Depending on what's playing and the deals negotiated, the tablet might have iMDB data about the program, stats and line-ups for a sporting event, additional content that's relevant to the show (e.g., text articles to supplement a news story), even ads that complement commercials being shown on the main screen. Everything will be tailored for that particular viewer, and here again the system will learn their preferences over time. So that if the viewer prefers to see photos along with a news story, they'll see that rather than text articles. And if they are participating in a second screen quiz around a game show, the app will automatically open the quiz once the viewer turns to that show.

TIED TO THE GRID

As previously discussed, there's an odd contractual quirk preventing the user experience on MVPD set-top boxes from improving. The broadcast networks pay to maintain the channel number they had back in the pre-cable days. So if the CBS station in New York City was channel 2 in 1975, it will continue to be channel 2 on the cable line-up and 502 in the HD channel line-up in 2015. Which means that the default view for the electronic program guides has to be the old-school grid, which on most systems now exceeds one thousand channels what with HD and subscription and music and international channels and all. That thousand-channel grid does not make for a pleasant user experience, especially not when the average viewer only watches about 10 to 20 channels. (To be fair, most systems do have some way to set up a favorites list, it's just not intuitive or publicized and requires more than a bit of googling to find some enterprising techie who's posted the instructions online.)

Numbering aside, the other logical way to lay out the grid, with stations alphabetized by name or by category, is rarely in sync with what the networks perceive to be fair. It gives an unfair advantage to Animal Planet and ABC, while YES and the Weather Channel get a perceived disadvantage. Then there's the debate on whether The Weather Channel gets alphabetized under "T" for "The" or "W" for "Weather." And when you've got 1,000 channels to scroll through, alphabetical order is only slightly less cumbersome than numerical.

My prediction is that the networks will eventually let go of this anachronism. *Eventually* being the key word, but they will. And the reason will be because they'll see that a guide that puts user experience and personalization first will actually get them more viewers than the position they had on the TV dial during the Carter administration.

Comcast has been the exception to the BYOD trend. Sort of. They're betting on their own set-top boxes, the X1 and the X2, but I say "sort of," because those boxes are a lot more like Roku and Apple TV (or an advanced version thereof) than they are like the old Scientific Atlanta boxes that keep the rest of the industry stuck in 1995. I've only heard positive things about X1s from friends who have them. Comcast's plan is to sell them to the other MVPDs and thus own the set-top box experience (and the profits that come along with it). Whether they'll be able to dominate—or whether their competitors will successfully make set-top box acquisition a consumer responsibility—has yet to play out, but my gut says we'll see a combination, and that the choice of set-top box may become a distinguishing feature, either between the MVPDs themselves or between the various options they give to consumers. So that a full cable customers may get either a set-top box or streaming device, but over-the-top only (V-POP) customer would be asked to download an app to their tablet or streaming device.

THE TIVO DILEMMA

No discussion of set-top boxes would be complete without looking at TiVo. The company burst on the scene in 1999 as a next-generation DVR that had features which (sadly enough) are still considered advanced today: algorithm-based recommendations, easy-to-use menus, automatic recordings of movies featuring a specific actor or around a specific topic. TiVo's business model never quite worked, though: by charging upwards of $200 for a box, with a monthly fee at around $20, it didn't stand a chance against the MVPD set-top boxes with built-in DVRs (less clutter) and charges that were cleverly buried inside the cable bill. While the company has limped along, buoyed in recent years by the proceeds of several multimillion dollar lawsuits, it seems fated to being overtaken on one side by the Comcast "X Boxes" and on the other side by the more nimble streaming devices. Which is too bad because they really do look at the experience from a completely consumer-centric POV. Unfortunately the business model never matched and consumers decided it wasn't worth the hassle.

APPS ON A FRAMEWORK

So what does the electronic program guide (EPG) of the future look like, regardless of what sort of a device it lives on? I'm thinking that what happens is that each network owns its own experience—something similar to what you currently see on their TVE apps—with the MVPDs providing a framework that allows you to search across all networks and use a universal VOD and DVR services. (If, indeed, there is a DVR. More on that in the next chapter.)

So you'll have a home screen that has recommended programming as the hero images (similar to the current Netflix or Hulu home pages) with your favorites/watch list second in the hierarchy, and a link to the electronic program guide in the third slot.

You'll be able to search the guide via voice commands and text input, but once you've found a show and clicked to watch it, you'll be taken into that network's world. Which may include secondary content (quizzes, polls, behind the scenes) accessed from the tablet or on-screen, links to watch other network shows, or cross-show promotions that the network is running. Everything on the network page will have a common design scheme so you'll be aware that you are watching CBS not Cartoon Network.

What this does is solve the problem of networks wanting to control their own experiences, the way they currently can on apps, without forcing consumers to download and then switch between dozens of individual apps to watch the shows they want. The networks' current pain point is the loss of brand identity (we've gone from NBC's "Must See TV" Thursday night line-up to "What network is that on?" in about 15 years.) And allowing them to build their own branded experience and have it live on the MVPD's EPG is the perfect solution.

It also works for the MVPDs, whose pain point is that they'll quickly be turned into just another pipe and made irrelevant. In this model, they get to own the data generated by users and the greater interface. All of which saves them from being irrelevant.

Finally, it works for consumers, who get the best of both worlds: the ease of searching a universal menu with the full array of content—both primary and supplementary—that a network site can offer.

And if you're thinking that this sort of guide sounds great and why hasn't anyone invented it yet, the answer is that it's all about rights and getting the networks to accept the fact that they need to share the MVPDs' program guides with streaming services. At least that's what we heard when I was at Piksel and was shopping around an earlier prototype of this called the "Social Program Guide" that had all of these features. It will get here, just give it time.

RECOMMENDATION AND DISCOVERY

Recommendation engines will play a huge role in helping consumers make their way through the mass of content, both from traditional TV companies and from new players who release series online. Recommendation engines will be one of the ways in which pay TV providers will distinguish themselves, providing better and easier ways to find shows to watch. (versus the current paradigm, which is still "We have more channels").

Finding something to watch on TV was a lot simpler in the pre-cable days. There were three networks, PBS, and possibly an independent station or two. Your choices were limited to whatever they had on at the time. Suffice it to say people spent a lot of time watching shows they had zero interest in. (Which begat the habit of using the TV as background noise, but that's its own story.)

Today's landscape is very different: there is a broad selection of TV shows and movies available on streaming services and VOD, not to mention several hundred linear broadcast channels, and the decision of what to watch gets a lot more complicated. It's not just *what* to watch, but where to watch it and how much—do you just want one episode or are you looking for a new series to binge-view?

Hence the value of recommendations and suggestions.

While the terms *Suggestion Engine* and *Recommendation Engine* are used interchangeably, they actually refer to two very different behaviors and desired outcomes.

A suggestion engine is for those times when we have a fairly specific idea of what we want and are in active search mode.

A recommendation engine is for when we're done watching TV; it basically says, "Here are some things you might enjoy the next time you decide to watch TV."

That distinction shows that the suggestion engine is far more valuable because it comes into play in response to an active request on the part of the user. A recommendation engine is far more passive; the user is not actively looking for any additional input: if the engine shows them something that they wind up being interested in, that's just a lucky strike extra.

To put a real world face on these terms, Jinni, the Israeli software company, offers a good example of a suggestion engine: you give it input (e.g., "I'm looking for a comedy set in England in the 1960s") and it will come back at you with a list of movies that meet that criteria that you can access immediately. If you've included social graph data, it can indicate which of those movies your friends have watched and what they thought of them. There's an expectation from both the user and the software that the suggestion will be acted on immediately.

Amazon's various "You might also like" engines are a good example of recommendation engines: while you may be on the site to buy a teapot for your great-aunt, it's possible you might also see a book on tea in the "You might also like" list that intrigues you. It's also possible you'll go straight for the teapot: there's no expectation from either party that the recommendation will be acted on.

A subtle distinction, but an important one.

SOCIAL RECOMMENDATIONS

Social graphs don't always make for the best recommendation engines because the people we're connected to on social networks don't necessarily consist of our friends as much as a random collection of people from various points in our lives, some of whom we may also be related to. And because social media behavior itself is often random, it's often inaccurate: people will "like" a whole bunch of movies when they first join Facebook but won't bother to Like any current movies. Or they'll Like something because it somehow showed up in their timeline, while movies they actually liked much better go unremarked upon. Twitter provides even less guidance because the user base is much smaller— it's rare that all of someone's friends are on Twitter, rarer still that the friends who are using the platform are all active users. So while there may be some value in learning what the mass of Twitter users are talking about and which shows are getting the most tweets, it's sort of like determining what music to listen to based on the Billboard 100—useful at some level, but not overly discriminating.

The real value in discovery engines, be they suggestion or recommendation engines—is that they restore the notion of serendipity and helps us find titles we would otherwise not have been aware of. That's important because serendipity is what gets lost in an online world, and that makes it harder for new works to get discovered and for us to stumble onto things outside our comfort zone. That may not be the immediate reason we like them: a good discovery engine just makes it easy to navigate through the muck. Still, it's nice to know they have a value beyond that.

Serendipity is going to be more important too as the pool of available content expands. Right now, most recommendations are obvious: if you like *Big Bang Theory* you'll probably like (or at least be very aware of) *How I Met Your Mother*, *The Office*, *Seinfeld*, *Parks and Recreation* and other hit sitcoms of the late 90s and early 00s and 10s. But as the pool of well-produced, available content expands—something we already see in the movie choices that are available to us—so does the ability of the system to surprise you with something you were previously unaware of.

META-TAGGING

One thing that the industry will need to work on in order to make discovery engines more effective is meta-tagging. Meta tags are descriptors attached to a piece of content that search engines use to determine relevancy. Right now, too many shows and movies, especially older ones, don't have more than basic tagging (e.g., comedy, drama, etc). That's something Netflix has taken the lead on, by hiring hundreds of people who watch and tag these shows relying on a 36-page manual that offers tips on how and why to categorize them. The result is that Netflix now has around 76,897 different types of tags for content. Which is what allows them to offer up all those quirky category titles, but also helps tremendously with the science behind them. When the rest of the industry catches up, discovery will be far more precise, with the system able to really fine-tune its suggestions and offer them up to you in a way a really good librarian or bookstore clerk might. The ideal being, "Here's something you've never heard of, but I suspect you'll really like."

And just as in real life, lots of people will demur, will go for the safer, more comfortable choice. But those who don't will be richly rewarded.

NON-SKIPPABLE VOD

While much has been made lately over cloud-based DVR services, there's another line of thinking that says the DVR may soon be heading the way of the 8-track.

Its killer? Non-skippable VOD.

While consumers may love their DVRs, no one on the industry side has ever been particularly fond of them. DVRs allow viewers to miss live broadcasts and, more important, skip commercials. And even if they're not skipping commercials, they're often watching ones that are out of date, their offers having expired, the movie no longer in theaters.

As the networks have come to terms with the whole notion of binge-viewing and making everything available on VOD pretty much immediately, they've also come to realize the financial advantage VOD has over DVR.

With VOD, the networks control the interaction. With DVR, it's the consumer. That means the networks can ensure that their VOD programming has non-skippable commercial slots built into it. And that allows them to continue the current ad-supported television model, possibly even growing it, as VOD also offers the opportunity for dynamic ad insertion—placing ads in those non-skippable slots based on what is known about the consumer, their buying habits, their taste in shows, their location, and the time and day of the week. Which means those VOD slots can become even more valuable than live ones.

And so look to the networks to push the MVPDs who will gladly stick a fork in the DVR. Something they can easily do because other than TiVo, there just aren't that many independent DVR manufacturers. Most people have their DVR through their cable box, and if the MVPDs want to kill it off, they pretty much can. Which won't be that big a deal for consumers if every show is instantly available on VOD. In fact, most people might find VOD a more convenient setup as they'll no longer have to worry about recording things or whether the football game ran longer than it was supposed to and knocked everything else off schedule.

The catch, of course, is that the networks can't get too greedy. If they stick to a couple of Hulu-esque 60- or 90-second commercial pods, they will be fine and consumers won't get all that hot and bothered about the commercial breaks. But if they get greedy and insist on eight minutes worth of commercials on every 30-minute prime-time show (the current on-air ratio), then I'd look to buy stock in TiVo and anyone else who still makes a DVR.

It's a tough call too, because there's such a built-in bias towards greed, towards discounting what the consumer wants because previously, the consumer didn't have any other options.

Once again, time will tell.

NEW BUSINESS MODELS

One of the most interesting things about the growth of technology options is that there's suddenly a new range of different business models that may prove as viable or more viable than the current ones. In this chapter, we'll take a look at some of them and how they might play out.

MAYBE THE MODEL WITH ADS IS THE LESS DESIRABLE OPTION

Once you've gotten used to watching television without advertising, it's really hard to go back.

That's something the industry hasn't really come to terms with yet—the fact that they've been training a whole generation (and many of its elders) to studiously avoid the very thing they use to pay the bills. It's like having a dull ache in your leg for years and then suddenly finding a pill that makes it go away. It wasn't life-altering pain, but once it's gone, you realize how much better you feel without it, and there's no way you're ever going to put up with it again.

I was thinking about this while listening to a recent Netflix earnings call. By charging eight dollars a month, Netflix is able to make hundreds of millions of dollars a year off subscriber fees alone. Without running commercials. Ever.

But how many networks are there that we'd pay eight dollars a month for? I suspect not that many. Maybe five or ten at most. The rest we could live without: we mostly watch them because they're free or we're bored or because they have one particular show we like. The rest is just a flyover zone, the channels you pass through when clicking from NBC to Showtime.

So here's a radical thought: what if we turned the whole paradigm around? What if we made ad-supported TV the back-up option and subscription services the premier one?

Take the CBS series *Under The Dome* which premiered on CBS in summer 2013 on Monday nights with multiple commercial breaks and then resurfaced on Fridays on Amazon, commercial free.

What if the process was reversed and the Monday-night broadcast was on a service called CBS Prime that you paid $8/month to subscribe to and where you got to watch *Under The Dome* and other CBS series ad-free?

Viewers who didn't sign up for CBS Prime would get to watch the show five days later for free, only with the usual eight minutes-worth of advertising thrown in.

This would create two strong reasons for fans to subscribe to CBS Prime (early access and no commercials) and would still allow the show to build audience with remaining viewers, some of whom might like the show enough to sign up for CBS Prime. It would also place pressure on the networks to improve the quality of their programming so that viewers would want to sign up for the prime versions.

There are potential downsides to this maneuver: affluent audiences might just default to the ad-free services and be lost to advertisers forever (though I'd argue that this is more or less happening already, thanks to streaming, VOD, and DVR.)

The industry would also be forced to admit that an ad-supported model is an inferior model and risk losing ad revenue. (Though again, you can argue that this is already the case with apps and it's not hurting mobile ad revenue. Plus TV advertising still has incredible reach, and services that tie TV spots to mobile ads can help extend that reach, while also hitting affluent audiences.) The networks also risk offending advertisers by hinting at the fact that viewers didn't really like advertising: the whole ad-supported model is based on the myth that consumers are happy to watch "relevant" or "engaging" brand messages. For real.

The biggest downside, though, would be that the Prime system would only work for a dozen networks at most, and that would create a more transparent two-tier system. On the other hand, if costs were low enough and a niche network had a small-but-extremely-loyal following, the Prime system could work for them as well. And as we've seen earlier, niche content with a supportive audience can be a successful endeavor.

How it would work is also open for discussion: the most logical move would be an HBO-style service with a preset linear schedule, though there's also an argument to be made for a pure VOD service that had much of the network's library already on it (ad-free) and where each new episode would be available for download at noon Eastern time on Mondays. A Netflix-style system where all episodes were released at once is also possible, though spoilers might serve to disincentivize weekly viewers.)

Given that studies show most viewers are no longer watching their favorite shows live (and are thus presumably watching them without commercials) a shift in emphasis to align TV with the rest of the entertainment industry—where the free/ad-supported model—is not the preferred model, could go a long way toward keeping those viewers happy and keep them from leaving the pay TV ecosystem. It's a major paradigm shift, but it's one that could work to the advantage of all parties involved. Viewers in particular.

AVOIDING THE MIDDLEMAN

One of the more interesting things I've been hearing about lately hasn't been about improving the current environment but, rather, avoiding it.

It seems numerous people have allegedly done the math in their heads and come up with a Hollywood elevator pitch that goes something like this: "House of Cards. Without the middleman."

The idea is that there's a lot of talent in Hollywood, but that talent rarely makes it past the gatekeepers. And that networks like AMC, HBO, Showtime and now Netflix have proven that if you assemble the most talented writers and directors in the industry and let them follow their vision, you get award-winning shows, and a whole lot of buzz, which eventually translates to a whole lot of money. And then Netflix proved that you can put those well-crafted shows online and still get that buzz. To which the next logical response seemed to be "Well then, who needs Netflix?"

So the idea is to raise the money to produce a high-quality show: top writers, top actors, large production budgets. Only then, instead of selling it to a network (or wannabe network), you put it online yourself. Via a Roku channel, an Xbox app, an iPad app, and a website. By selling subscriptions or advertising or a little of both you can recoup the money you spent producing and marketing the show and then some—more than you would have gotten from selling it to a network or Netflix, with the potential for a lot more, as the long-tail effect kicks in along with overseas licensing deals.

The trick is going to be getting enough people to look at it to make the venture worthwhile. Because what's the most important thing a network does for a show? It markets the hell out of it. Via on-air promotions. Press junkets. Billboards on the sides of busses. Fan outreach. And if you're going to go it alone, you're going to need to find a way to replicate all of that. In a way that ensures that your ad revenue less your marketing spend is still a very attractive number.

Social media can help. Because if your stars or your show have large social media followings, then they can use those followers to help drive views. (Remember Scott Lowell's comment in the chapter on fan communities about casting decisions being influenced by an actor's Twitter following.) It's something we've been seeing for a while with YouTube stars who more or less exclusively use social media to drive their audiences. And when a YouTube star like Michelle Phan has 1.5 million Instagram followers and almost 600,000 Twitter followers, it's easy to see where those eyeballs are coming from and why her videos routinely get well over a million views.

There's a distinct first mover advantage to allowing social media to drive your traffic. Fans will happily serve as advertising vehicles until they won't, until the time when it seems like everyone is asking them to promote something or other and they just shut down. We've seen it happen already: the first brands on Twitter got a whole lot of traction because they were there first. People couldn't believe that Tony Hsieh, the CEO of Zappos, was actually talking to them online. But by the time the 80th CEO showed up, the notion was no longer novel, and the whole thing seemed fake and contrived.

Which brings us back to the Achilles' heel of relying on fans: authenticity. If fans feel like they're being manipulated or played, they shut down and stop playing along. Which is why the key to any play that relies on social media has got to be maintaining authenticity and speaking to fans with honesty and respect. It's also got to be part of who your stars are: not every celebrity is built to be a non-stop self-promotion machine, and if a normally reticent actor starts to sound like a Kardashian, fans are going to call bullshit.

Which is not to say it's impossible to build a successful independent site where you sell directly to fans on an ad-supported model. Far from it. But for most projects, social media marketing alone won't be enough. Paid marketing and promotions will have to be a key part of the model, along with top-notch user experience and design.

Even with all that, it's far from a sure thing: you'd really need to get a lot of viewers or advertisers paying a lot of money to make something like this turn a profit. But if you did—or even if you almost did—the shockwaves reverberating through the industry would look a lot like Wile E. Coyote after the anvil fell on him.

THE END OF AFFILIATES AND O&Os

This is a long-term prediction (say ten years) but I don't see most local stations surviving the digital era. There's just no need for them when viewers get their TV directly from the networks wherever and whenever they want. Local stations made sense in an era of broadcast TV when all stations were local. But, when everything is delivered over the internet, they make a lot less sense: viewers can get any and all types of programming they want online or via their set-top box (though the distinction between the two will soon be nil). So there's no need for a local station except for local news, which can be handled by any number of web or VOD based providers who supply local news that can be accessed at any time. Larger markets may be able to support 24-hour news stations, but for smaller markets, two half-hour shows a day, available on demand, will be all that is needed. And that will mark the slow demise of the local television station. There will be survivors, though—stations that, like Chicago's WGN, manage to market themselves to a national audience and those that manage to gain fans with a strong regional audience, perhaps focusing on college or high school sports and local news. But those stations will be few and far between. The rest will be casualties of the shifting television landscape.

THE RISE OF MCNs

MCNs (multi channel networks)—online only networks which serve as alternates to pay TV and generally feature short form content—have emerged as the golden children of the past year or two. And so we're witnessing things that would have been unheard of just a few years back, things like Disney buying Maker Studios (one of the most popular MCNs) and Endemol, the world's largest independent TV production company, launching Endemol Beyond, its own version of an MCN. There's even Vessel, with $75 million of VC funding, attempting to take on YouTube by luring away its biggest stars, promising them a greater share of the profits if they'll give the platform a 72-hour window on exclusive content.

While categories like music, fashion, and comedy tend to do well in this arena as they lend themselves to short-form content, the biggest surprise (to those on the outside, anyway) are sites like Machinima and Twitch which cater to gamers. But not, as you might expect, with game reviews and previews of new games. What Machinima and Twitch mainly feature are videos of people *playing* games, a genre known as "eSports." Sure they'll sometimes reveal tips and tricks, but the real thrill is in watching the play, in much the same way baseball fans like seeing the Red Sox and Yankees play. This has come as a real surprise to those outside of the gaming community. Especially when Google is reported to be offering over $1 billion to buy Twitch, a spin-off from Justin.TV (a site originally notable as a place to watch pirated streams of live sports broadcasts). But it's real and it's huge and it's all user-generated.

Which is another thing about the MCNs: Most of their biggest stars, like PewDiePie and the aforementioned Michelle Phan, who does her own beauty and make-up show, are people shooting their own stuff and putting them up on YouTube where, due to a combination of talent, clever promotion, and luck, they've gained a huge fan base. How huge? *Variety* did a study on teens in summer 2014, showing them YouTube stars like Phan and Smosh and A-list celebrities that appeal to the teen demographic like Katie Perry and Jennifer Lawrence. The result was very surprising: the YouTube stars were as well if not better known than the Hollywood stars. That's a real game changer.

The rise of MCNs has attracted filmmakers who aren't full-on A-list pros but aren't rank amateurs either. They're looking at sites like Funny Or Die, with videos written, produced, and starring pro talent and realizing that online could very easily become the farm team for pay TV or the place that programs with strong niche audience go to retire.

Which is exactly how I think it is going to play out. A 15-minute web-only series (and there are plenty of them already) is only seven minutes shorter than a 22-minute sitcom (22 minutes of show plus eight minutes of commercials.) And so it's quite conceivable that online video could become a farm system for pay TV, where success looked like a slightly longer format, a bigger production budget, and more money for paid promotion.

There are advantages to this system for all parties. The creators obviously get more money. But they are also able to build up an international audience (web video has no geo-restrictions) which is going to be a powerful negotiating tool down the road when it comes to selling valuable foreign rights.

The system can also work in reverse: a show that does not get good ratings on pay TV but has a dedicated fan base can live on as a web series and potentially make the same amount of money for its creators, thanks to the passion of the fan base.

Those working in that segment see a very bright future indeed. "Describing these companies as 'multi-channel networks' will soon sound as quaint as 'new media'," notes David B. Williams, Content and Strategy Director at Endemol Beyond. "Whether through evolution or acquisition, today's MCNs are becoming modern multi-faceted media companies."

Multi-faceted media companies with the ability to quickly monetize their stars' popularity. As the aforementioned *Variety* study brought to light, many YouTube stars have audiences that Hollywood stars can only envy.

Take Cameron Dallas, for instance. Dallas is a 20 year-old Vine star, a good looking kid who often appears shirtless in his six second videos. Which is a polite way of saying his audience consists mostly of middle school-aged girls. Millions of middle school-aged girls. 7.6 million on Vine, 6.4 million on Instagram, 4.8 million on Twitter, 3.6 million on YouTube, and 2.1 million on Facebook, to be exact.

Last summer, Awesomeness.tv, the MCN Dallas works with, decided to put him in a movie. The film, called *Expelled* (loosely modeled after *Ferris Bueller's Day Off*), was greenlit shortly before Labor Day. It was shot during October, post-production took place in November, and the film had a limited theatrical release the week before Christmas.

On December 26, 2014, *Expelled* was released on DVD and VOD, and within twelve hours it knocked *Guardians of the Galaxy* off the number one slot on iTunes. The marketing budget was minimal. All those millions of fans found out about the film via social media. And while Dallas is the exception rather than the rule, he's far from the only social media star capable of commanding these sort of numbers. Something mainstream Hollywood should most definitely be taking note of.

BLURRED LINES

The other thing web video has going for it is that the lines between "TV" and "Video" are rapidly blurring, especially for the younger generation, which has grown up with both. As production quality for "video" improves and the availability of "TV" on devices other than a TV becomes commonplace, it will be more difficult to tell one from the other. The difference between those who make money and those who don't will always boil down to the ability to draw an audience, and video stars, whose audiences have sprung up organically and are sustained by social media, will find themselves in a very good position.

Which is not to say that shows like *Game of Thrones* with its multimillion-dollar-per-episode production budget will go away.

Just that there will be far more gray area between that and a three minute home video posted by two high school kids.

Making money off of web video is another issue, as YouTube takes a notoriously large percentage of profits (45% of ad revenue) while providing a hugely successful (and free) discovery tool for video content producers. Hence the rise of the MCNs, which give successful video stars a place to grab a much larger share of advertising revenue without losing their audiences.

"The key insight about the business of YouTube is that audiences are as abundant as profits are scarce," explains Endemol Beyond's Williams. "That means approaching YouTube as a highly efficient, potentially self-liquidating marketing platform. It brings to mind how the movie studios shifted their approach to theatrical distribution, now viewing it as an occasionally profitable loss-leader that elevates the entire lifecycle of a filmed property across home video, foreign distribution, licensing, merchandising, etc. Where YouTube was once a place to build a business, today it is seen as a place to secure a beachhead."

In other words, it's a whole new ballgame

While YouTube has its limitations, there's a whole crew of players who sit between YouTube and network TV, companies like Netflix, Hulu, Amazon, AOL, Sony, Microsoft, and Yahoo who have the budgets the TV networks have but deliver their video programming online. It's not too much of a stretch to imagine Apple, Google, and Facebook joining that list, creating their own high-production-value original programming.

And that's where the lines really get blurry. Because if Netflix is already competing with HBO for series (*House of Cards*), and those series are then being sold in supermarkets as DVDs (*House of Cards* again) it won't be long before we see syndication deals and overseas rights deals being struck, and then the only difference between the larger online players and the traditional players is that the latter are stuck in the linear delivery mode. For now, at least. (The following chapter on Spotifyization explains all that.)

Equally important, the talent who makes those series—the actors, writers, producers and directors—will be able to continue making a living creating shows for the larger online players.

"I think the initial burst of new opportunities that were there for writers in new media, whether it was creating a great one-off sketch for *Funny or Die* or a regular web series on YouTube, was great for getting some new writers attention and serving as a calling card for them and their talent that could impress the gatekeepers of old media (smart people at the networks looking for new voices)." notes Alan Dybner, who wrote the *Café Attitude* skit for *Funny or Die* mentioned in the chapter on fandom. "But on its own, creating content for new media was very rarely directly profitable for the writer in the way getting staffed on a network show could be, with some very notable exceptions (like the super-talented Felicia Day)," he added.

Dybner, who has been a staff writer for several series, including *That 70s Show*, sees much more opportunity in the larger online players. "Now, with Netflix, Amazon, Hulu, Yahoo, Google, Sony Playstation, etc. getting into funding bigger and bigger original projects, it seems like new media might become another place where a writer can make a living," he says. "Not by the writer trying to use their online project as a calling card to get hired at the broadcast or cable networks, but by finding their own audience online, one that doesn't need to be as enormous as a broadcast or cable network, and that might allow new types of storytelling that don't have to fit into the same time and content constraints as current television. This only works if these online series are covered by the WGA [Writers Guild of America—the union for television writers] from the get go, to make sure the writers of these projects who aren't already established names (so not your Sorkins or Dan Harmons) get a fair deal and can make a livable wage with benefits and residual payments and a percentage of the back end should their show be a hit. Which would be very different than what happened to the last group of writers to work in new territory, the writers of 'reality' TV, who continue to get none of these benefits despite being the main creative force behind the shows they work on."

Dybner's last point is critical; in order for Hollywood to continue to draw the type of talent it's been drawing—the top writers, actors and directors—it needs to be able to pay them for top-line original content. And that is far more likely to happen with the larger online players, who can bring in the same size audiences—and potentially more ad revenue—than even the largest premium cable or broadcast networks.

It would also save the television industry from the sad fate of print journalism, where an explosion of free online outlets like the Huffington Post has driven down the value of writers (and the quality of writing) and is starting to drive away top talent. Which may become a vicious cycle: if the most talented writers are driven to where the money is (Hollywood), print will become even more devalued. Until, of course, it hits rock bottom and there's a demand for quality again.

But that's a whole other story.

THE SPOTIFYIZATION OF TELEVISION

In the broad curve of technological change, the music industry has, for better and for worse, always been a few years ahead of the television industry. And while the very different business models between the two industries translates to very different disruption models, if you want to see where the future of television will net out, you need to look no further than Spotify.

Spotify provides the answer to the question of how we're going to be watching TV: will everything be on demand, with viewers sifting through a huge catalog of shows to find something to watch that night? Or will there still be linear TV, where all the viewer is required to do is hit the "on" button and sink back on the couch?

The answer, judging from the success of Spotify and similar services, is both.

Spotify works because it solves all of the various use-case scenarios its audience might have.

If you feel like listening to a specific song, Spotify lets you do that, even providing alternate and cover versions.

Feel like listening to a playlist you've made yourself, the latter-day version of the mixtape? You can do that too.

Have a friend with really great taste in music and want to listen to their playlists? All you need to do is subscribe—the latter-day version of the gifted mixtape.

And finally, if you just want someone else to take over the controls, Spotify provides a variety of curated "radio stations" either through the app or via third-party providers like SoundCloud and Rolling Stone.

So if we look at how this plays out in television, we'll soon see a very similar array of options.

1. VIDEO ON DEMAND (VOD). If there's a particular show or movie you want to watch, you'll be able to do a quick search and call it up. This will also allow for binge viewing, as you'll be able to watch an entire season at once or just the four episodes that you missed. VOD viewing can be a quick half-hour surgical strike, or a long evening of catch-up—whatever suits your mood.

2. PLAYLISTS. Viewers will have their own playlists of TV series they are in the midst of watching, movies they've flagged for future viewing, and/or repeats of their favorite shows. These will function like music playlists—one show plays right after the next, so there's no need to go back to the program guide after every episode.

3. CURATED PLAYLISTS. These can be from friends or from professional curators and may be around a specific topic: best crime dramas, best of CSI, best of 90s sitcoms—the possibilities are endless. Viewers can watch the entire playlist at once or just work their way through the list one at a time.

4. LINEAR STATIONS. These will function much like the "radio" stations on music services today and will in large part be curated by today's cable and broadcast networks. They will have original, first-run content that's aired at a specific day and time. Users will be able to personalize them by, say, emphasizing certain types of content (e.g., comedies), but some version of prime time will remain in effect because there's still a lot of love for a shared communal live viewing experience beyond just news and sports.

5. PERSONALIZED LINEAR STATIONS. These will be the oft-cited "Pandora for TV"—the viewer inputs some of the shows or types of shows they like and an algorithm puts together a personalized linear station for them, a combination of live broadcast, VOD, and non-broadcast video from alternative providers. Users will be able to set up linear stations for short-form content, long-form content or both.

6. PERSONALIZED ACCOUNTS. While Spotify's pay service is still in its nascency, we can see the outlines of how a system

works where users are charged according to the number of devices they wish to access and the number of individual users they want on each account. This is the wave of the future, and while it may not result in any significant financial savings for consumers, it will (finally) enable the roll out of true TV Everywhere.

As with the current music services, how you watch will vary depending on your mood, your time commitment. even your personality. There are people who love the randomness of Pandora, others who want to control their entire listening experience, and every variation in between. TV will work the same way and the truth is many of us are already watching it this way: bingeing on series via VOD or streaming services like Amazon, watching live sporting events or NBC's Thursday night line-up, supplementing our pay-TV subscriptions with Netflix, Hulu, and other streaming services.

PERSONALIZATION AND MONETIZATION

Personalization will be the buzzword as everyone will have their own TV service that travels with them no matter what device they're watching on. Viewers will have the ability to associate specific playlists with a specific device, such as their mobile phones or tablets, to enable viewing that's appropriate to the environment they're in when they watch on that device (on a train, in the office, etc.).

Recommendations will be key in this new world too, as viewers are looking for new shows to add to existing playlists, new playlists to add to their rotation, and new shows on linear channels that become "appointment TV" for them.

Monetization will be key to enabling this new world, and the solution is likely to come in two forms: (a) dynamically inserted ad units that run using algorithms that factor in time of day, location, what show is being watched, and the user's prior behavior, and (b) straight-up fees which will enable a viewer to watch an entire series without commercial interruption or to access special super-premium content that's above and beyond the usual fare.

The operators who run these multi-platform systems will differentiate themselves the same way the music services currently do: variations in the interface and user experience. To wit, the hand-curated playlists on the Beats Music service is something that could easily be adapted to television and give whoever offered those playlists a competitive advantage.

The future of television isn't far off, but unlike the music industry, it's not going to change overnight. There are too many legal restrictions, too many complicated rights issues, too much legacy equipment in the field to see the sort of rapid metamorphosis we've seen in other media industries.

It will change, though, and the challenge now is to actually enable that change.

A NEW REVENUE MODEL

Netflix and other subscription services are training an entire generation to watch television without commercials, which is ironic given that the bulk of their offering consists of TV series whose very existence was made possible by the revenue from said commercials.

Netflix's Reed Hastings stumbled on to what appeared to be a winning formula several years back: having lost the Starz catalogue, and the current movies that came with it, he approached the various networks and studios and offered to pay millions of dollars for the rights to older seasons of their current shows, many which were sitting on the shelf waiting for the series to hit the magic 100-episode mark needed for syndication.

What initially seemed a win-win proposition is now a dangerous trend for both parties: by weaning audiences from live viewing and teaching them to binge on their own schedule, all without commercials, Netflix is killing the goose that laid the golden egg. While audiences are watching more television than ever, they're watching less of it live, causing ad revenue to shrink.

A big part of the problem is an ad-buying system built around live viewing and the Nielsen ratings to measure it. Despite mounting evidence that viewers have been abandoning live viewing, Nielsen has not produced a viable system for counting all those non-linear views. That mistake is compounded by the ad industry's inability to work out how to serve up a similarly robust ad load for all those VOD and streaming views, which it tends to discount by lumping them all under the catch-all term "digital."

Even more problematic is that much non-linear viewing now takes place on DVRs, where people skip through ads. NBC's research chief recently noted that if DVRs were their own network, they'd be four times the size of the four largest U.S. TV networks combined. Given viewers' strong preference for watching TV on their own schedules, DVR viewing numbers are only going to rise.

That is a problem. If viewers continue to avoid the advertising that is the television industry's bread and butter, ad revenue is going to start to dry up and along with it, the money to fund production of new TV shows. So, what are the alternatives? How is the industry going to replace some of that $65 billion in annual revenue?

There are several options. Branded content, either as part of the main programming schedule or as part of a second screen effort, is the most talked-about alternative. Given the ubiquity of branded content and so-called native advertising in other online media, audiences should not prove overly resistant to its introduction on TV. The trick, as always, is to make sure that the "content" part is more important than the "branded" part, so that what is produced is something people actually want to watch, not a 15- or 30-minute infomercial. Entertaining programming is entertaining programming, no matter who funds it.

We saw the first attempt at this during the Grammys this year, as retailer Target bought up eight adjacent 30-second spots to create a four-minute block, during which they ran a live concert by the band Imagine Dragons. The band was not up for a Grammy, but Target bet on the fact that music fans would rather see a live concert from a popular band than a series of interruptive ads.

They were right, and we're going to start seeing a lot more branded content like this.

Branded promotions are another option. Shows can partner with brands to create sponsored promotional vehicles for the show that also help boost awareness for the brand. The "halo effect" of being associated with a viewer's favorite program can be valuable to brands. The bigger and more active a show's fan base is, the more valuable it is to potential sponsors. That's why showrunners will need to continue reaching out to fans on social media and providing even greater support for fan communities.

Another way networks will recover the missing ad revenue is by leasing their programs to more platforms. The social networks have looked on in envy as Netflix gained millions of subscribers and, more important, the data associated with them. It is very likely that Facebook, YouTube, and even Twitter will want to license network programming, using the vast storehouse of knowledge they have about their users to match the right people to the right programming.

The larger legacy platforms such as Yahoo and AOL will also get in on the action—both have already begun to explore creating their own original programming, and Yahoo has purchased rights to the recently cancelled NBC show *Community*.

The trick for the networks will be to play the various platforms against each other, so that they continue to get top dollar for their shows.

Finally, as we'll see in the next chapter, if interruptive advertising wants a place in this new ecosystem, it will need to become much less intrusive and far more targeted. That's where personalized viewing will come into play. The data that's collected will allow for very targeted advertising that the networks can then charge more for. The result will be fewer but more relevant commercials, a combination that should convince viewers to stick around for the commercial breaks.

While I can't guarantee that these options will be enough to make up for all the advertising revenue the television industry stands to lose, the fallout may actually be a boon for audiences: tighter budgets will force networks to produce shorter seasons of higher quality programming that attract the sort of very involved fan bases that allow for the growth of alternative revenue streams.

Stranger things have happened.

THE CONTINUED DOMINANCE OF DATA

One of the few things we can be sure of as the television industry evolves over the next decade is that data will be the driving force behind decision making on everything from programming choices to ad serving to casting. The danger is that we become too reliant on data and forget the value of intuition.

While our current system is largely inefficient, it is driven by human decisions based in large part on guesswork and instinct. What data we do use, primarily focus groups and similar testing, is highly suspect and tends to reward content that appeals to the lowest common denominator. There are some who'd argue that's what people want, but I believe most people don't know what they want until they see it in front of them.

I witnessed the absurdity of testing firsthand during the years I worked in advertising. TV commercials were often tested via something called "animatics"—rough animations of the spots with agency employees (non-actors) reading the dialog and voiceovers. People who had accepted anywhere from 20 to 100 dollars to sit in a darkened auditorium were then asked their opinions of them.

The main problem (and there were many) with the methodology is that it doesn't take into account casting. Imagine being shown an animatic of the "Frankly, Scarlet, I don't give a damn," scene in *Gone With The Wind,* with the lines being read in a flat tone by non-actors. Without Clark Gable and Vivien Leigh to bring it to life, that scene probably just lies there. But add in the actors and it becomes one of the most memorable film moments of all time.

So that's the danger of data: relying on it so much that common sense and intuition are thrown out the window. And it's possible for this to occur, because in an industry that relies so heavily on subjective decisions made by fallible humans, the temptation to fall in love with an ostensibly objective decision-making process is a strong one.

The upside of data is that we can now track so many things we used to have to guess at, including exactly how many people are watching a certain show at a certain time, how long they've been watching it, where, and on what device. That's the sort of data that's helpful, as we can use it to see patterns and trends and make better decisions as a result.

If most of a show's audience watches it on an iPad at home within two hours of the show's initial airing, that calls for a marketing plan that's very different than the one used for a show that's mostly watched live, in a group, on a large-screen home TV.

The problem with that is, of course, Nielsen and the Nielsen Ratings, which the advertising community continues to cling to. I often liken it to *Let's Make A Deal*, the erstwhile 1970s game show. The advertisers have a Barcalounger, the current Nielsen ratings. And they could trade it in for what's behind Door Number Two (the actual ratings.) But what's behind Door Number Two could either be a donkey or a sports car, depending on whether their actual numbers are better or worse than the Nielsen numbers. And since they've already got the Barcalounger, they're not going to risk trading it in for a donkey.

This will change, too: either Nielsen will adapt and start relying on actual ratings (versus diary-based ratings), or someone will come in and steal their thunder. (Companies like Rentrak and Comscore are patiently waiting in the wings.) The pressure to start accurately gauging traffic, something that's commonplace in all other digital media, will be too strong to resist, and actual real-time ratings will become the norm.

While data can be used to make decisions on programming and how to market that programming to build and retain audiences, the data we'll soon be able to collect will be of greatest value to marketers. That's because we'll be able to know what commercials people watch, which ones they skip through, and which ones they interact with. It's also quite possible we'll be able to link that

161

information with their credit card purchase history so that we'll know what they eventually wind up buying, how much they spend on certain categories, what their favorite stores are, even what sites they visit most when browsing. That sort of information would, ostensibly, lead to better, more relevant, more targeted advertising that would be custom-tailored for you.

If only the whole notion wasn't so creepy.

People who sing the praises of this sort of consumer intelligence often forget that even though consumers may make all sorts of personal information available online, they're rarely thrilled when someone makes use of it. Partly because it seems like an invasion of privacy and partly because it's rarely ever accurate. We are not as predictable as the model makers would like to think. We are quirky and individualistic, and one of our least favorite things to hear is "This is who you are." Least of all from a perfect stranger.

That's why consumer data is going to be broader, and the value will be in being able to put advertising in front of more broadly defined targets, say, "women 18—24 who have watched a fashion ad four times more than average in the past month." That's a real number and it doesn't get down to the "We know you like Ann Taylor flats and black Elie Tahari skirts from Nordstrom so here's a coupon for each" weeds. As much as some in the tech community would want you to believe otherwise, there's not a whole lot of desire for that level of specificity, and it's what evokes the whole "Go away, you don't really know me" reaction.

LOCAL ADVERTISING

One small but unexpected bonus of big data is that it will allow local or even hyperlocal advertising to become part of the pay TV ecosystem. Your system will know where you are, what time of day it is and whether you are likely to be at work or at home. From there, it can offer ads for local shops and restaurants, hoping to entice people on their lunch breaks or on their way home. Here again, a balance has to be struck between useful and creepy as there is a fine line between the two. And it's going to be tough to keep on the right side of that line because there will be many advocating for the advantages of super refined targeting, for hitting people up with stalker-ish sounding messages from stores reminding them what they ate or purchased the last time.

PERSONALIZATION

At some very basic level people fall into two categories: those who like to fiddle with a device or an app, customizing all the settings, changing color schemes and menus, creating lists of favorites, and those who couldn't care less. The same will be true of future TV systems. Some people will go in and personalize them to the fullest extent possible, while others (most, I suspect) will leave the system settings as they are (lest they break them) and be happy when they're able to find something to watch faster than they were before.

It's also television. And as much as we want to make it something important, it's just television. Which for most people is not high on their list of priorities. They like being entertained, like the fact that TV can fill the voids and the lonely places. But it's still just the boob tube. Which means the less that we can be aware of *how* it's working and the more we can be aware of the fact that it *is* working, the more satisfied we will be.

And if the people who make the shows can use the data they gather from the people who watch the shows to make more money, chances are no one will begrudge them the opportunity.

So long as they're not all that aware that it's happening.

SUMMARY

So there you have it. The future of the television industry, circa spring 2015. Of course, I know enough to realize that by the time you read this, so many things may have already changed. (Go, updatable e-books!)

But some of the changes seem pretty certain to happen, no matter what else happens in the interim:

TV WILL BECOME UNMOORED from the traditional set-top box/TV set combination and be available on a range of devices in a range of places.

TV WILL BECOME MORE PERSONALIZED, with individual accounts replacing family accounts. This won't be a big deal for the millions of people who live alone and already have individual accounts, but the fact that your likes and preferences will follow you will make the whole experience easier and more seamless for the generation that starts out with these systems. (Think cell phones.)

TV WILL BECOME MORE DIVERSE. THERE will be more niche content supported by smaller, more passionate audiences. There will be 10-minute shows and two-hour shows and everything in between.

TV WILL BECOME MORE AVAILABLE. It already has. Thanks to streaming services, we can access a world of shows we once had to wait to see the rare times they showed up on syndication. And that trend will only continue as content owners realize that there's only upside to making shows and movies available online.

BINGE VIEWING IS HERE TO STAY. The combination of the second "Golden Age of Television" and the superior production quality thanks to HD means there's a world of content to be binge viewed by a generation that was too young to enjoy it when it was originally on the air.

OTHER THINGS ARE LESS CLEAR-CUT, the future of the pay-TV industry, in particular. Right now it looks pretty stable, and the MVPDs and the networks all seem to understand that they'll need to adapt to the new world order in order to survive. But how much they understand that and how much they'll let short-term greed stand in the way of long term viability remains to be seen.

Which is as good a thought as any to end this book on. Thanks for coming along for the ride.

-THE END-

ABOUT THE AUTHOR

As Senior Analyst for The Diffusion Group, Chairman of the 2nd Screen Society and Expert-In-Residence at BRaVe Ventures, Alan Wolk has become one of the industry's most influential thought leaders and futurists. He was recently recognized by *Wired* as one of the Top 20 Thinkers In Social TV and Second Screen.

His blog, The Toad Stool, is widely read and has become a forum for discussion around the changes coming from Hollywood, Silicon Valley, and beyond.

Wolk has written and spoken extensively about these upcoming changes and offers his insights on an exclusive basis for clients around the world via Toad Stool Consultants, where he provides bespoke advisory services for clients in the media and entertainment industries.

A frequent contributor to industry news sites, Wolk has been interviewed and quoted by everyone from NPR to *The Guardian* to *The New York Times* and recently appeared on a segment of public television's Brian Lehrer Show about the future of TV.

You can find Alan Wolk on Twitter at @awolk

Made in the USA
San Bernardino, CA
09 February 2018